Understanding Brecht

WALTER BENJAMIN

Translated by Anna Bostock

Introduction by Stanley Mitchell

VERSO

London · New York

First published as *Versuche über Brecht*
by Suhrkamp Verlag, 1966
© Suhrkamp Verlag, 1966
Poems by Bertolt Brecht © Stefan S. Brecht

Introduction first published, 1973
© Stanley Mitchell, 1973

First paperback edition 1977
Verso edition 1983
Second impression 1984
Third impression 1988
© NLB 1973

Verso
6 Meard Street, London W1
29 West 35th Street, New York, NY 10001-2291

Designed by Gerald Cinamon
Typeset in Monotype Fournier
and printed by
Thetford Press Limited
Thetford, Norfolk

ISBN 0 902308 99 8

Publisher's acknowledgment: We are grateful to Stefan S. Brecht and Eyre Methuen Ltd for their kind permission to reproduce the poems by Bertolt Brecht discussed in this book.

Translator's note: I have consulted the French edition, *Essais sur Brecht*, translated by Paul Laveau (François Maspero, Paris, 1967), and the translation of 'What is Epic Theatre?', by Harry Zohn, in *Illuminations* (Jonathan Cape and Harcourt Brace Jovanovich, London and New York, 1970), and of 'The Author as Producer', by John Heckman, in *New Left Review*, no. 62 (London, 1970).

Unless otherwise indicated all footnotes are taken from the German edition.

Benjamin had what Lukács so enormously
lacked, a unique eye precisely for significant
detail, for the marginal . . . for the impinging
and unaccustomed, unschematic particularity
which does not 'fit in' and therefore
deserves a quite special and incisive attention.
[ERNST BLOCH]

INTRODUCTION

Like Mayakovsky and the Russian Formalists,
Brecht and Benjamin form one of the classic literary partnerships of
the revolutionary Socialist movement. Their relationship, however,
is only now coming to light, for it was not until 1966 that the majority
of Benjamin's essays on Brecht were published.

Walter Benjamin was an eccentric 'man of letters', born of a well-
to-do German Jewish family in 1892. In the course of his lifetime,
he underwent a complex change, transposing the structures and
habits of his earlier mystical thought to enrich the categories of
Marxism.

Benjamin's idiosyncratic and difficult cast of mind blocked his
way to an academic career. Scholastic authorities rejected his doctoral
thesis (on the origins of German tragedy) for incomprehensibility.
But not only that: Benjamin, with characteristic lack of diplomacy,
had taken issue with Johannes Volkelt, one of the official aestheti-
cians of German academia. Barred from secure employment, he
became an itinerant man of letters, experiencing the intellectual
proletarianization he describes in 'The Author as Producer'. Had he

gained a university post it is difficult to say how his thought might have developed. With hindsight, many of his Marxist ideas are traceable in different forms to the days before his professional fate was decided. However, what is certain is that his precarious economic position sharpened his attraction to Marxism. At one point he contemplated joining the Communist Party.

The period was the late twenties and early thirties. Asya Lacis, a Communist theatrical producer, whom Benjamin had met in Capri in 1924, introduced him to Brecht whom he visited frequently during the thirties, staying with him for long periods during the latter's Danish exile. Throughout the decade, 1930 to 1939, responding to the rise and triumph of fascism, Benjamin wrote the present sketches and studies. Less fortunate than Brecht (luck was not one of his stars), Benjamin took his life in flight from the Gestapo, while attempting to cross the Franco-Spanish border in 1940.

Benjamin's writing is essayistic, aphoristic, fragmentary. Even his doctoral thesis is more a philosophical meditation than a systematic exposition and demonstration. At first it might seem odd that Brecht came together with Benjamin and not with someone more politically committed, Georg Lukács, for instance. But Brecht and Lukács never saw eye to eye. Whereas Lukács was hostile to the experimental art of the twentieth century because it lacked a sense of totality and perspective, Brecht shared with Benjamin a scavenging, magpie temperament, receptive to the often fragmented nature of modern art and literature. Benjamin was an extravagant collector and antiquarian, a passionate roamer and observer of cities, who could extract cultural histories from wayside odds and ends.

The diary extract, 'Conversations with Brecht', which concludes this volume, seems to show Brecht as the giver, Benjamin the taker; which was no doubt true psychologically. Benjamin's old Zionist friend, Gershom Scholem, wrote: 'Brecht was the harder nature and made a deep impact upon the more sensitive Benjamin who entirely lacked athletic qualities.' Intellectually, the relationship is certainly more complex and two-sided. There are, for instance, strong indications that the ideas and implications of 'epic theatre' were common to them both before they met.

This diary extract (never intended for publication) is so valuable because it gives the immediate atmosphere of the two men's conversations, their cast of mind, manner of speech, fondness for image, parable, allegory, aphorism, all of which we find separately in their writings. Whereas Benjamin was the more metaphorical thinker, from Brecht he learnt – what his former associates, from Gershom Scholem to T. W. Adorno, always deplored, considered disastrous – 'crude thinking' (*plumpes Denken*), that need for thought to simplify itself, crystallize out into essentials before it could be made practice.

Benjamin belonged to a generation of thinkers who, in the years just preceding the First World War, rebelled against the linguistic barrenness of German academic discourse. In different ways these thinkers sought to validate and discover meaning by revitalizing the semantic and metaphorical attributes of language itself. Marxism benefited from this generation in the writings of Benjamin, Bloch, and Adorno. At the same time, little will be gained from these Marxists, if they are approached with a 'commonsense', materialistic gauge. Here, as for poetry, one must follow Goethe's dictum:

> *Wer den Dichter will verstehen*
> *Muss in Dichters Lande gehen.*
> [If the poet you'd understand,
> You must go into the poet's land.]

With Benjamin it was the poet, Brecht, who was able to toughen the materialist sinews of the critic.

The Modern Sage

Two things, essentially, linked Brecht and Benjamin: a similar historical imagination and a similar humanism. Like Gramsci they were distinguished from the official Communist movement of the thirties by a deep historical pessimism into which, according to Romain Rolland's formula, 'Pessimism of the Intellect, Optimism of the Will', they planted seedlings of hope, and upon which they grounded a dialectical understanding of past and future. As with

Gramsci their pessimism was shaped by the victories of fascism. Germany seemed bent on its thousand-year empire. In addition, the degeneration of Socialism in the USSR quenched a hopeful attitude to the present.

The pessimism was strategic, designed to engender hope, not for foreseeable victories or reversals of fortune, but for the survival of the species as such. This was not yet the nuclear age, but Brecht spoke prophetically: 'They're planning for thirty thousand years ahead. . . . They're out to destroy everything. Every living cell contracts under their blows. . . . They cripple the baby in the mother's womb.' In his friend, Benjamin discovered 'a power that sprang from the depths of history no less deep than the power of the fascists'.

Brecht and Benjamin thought in millennia, geologically, of new dark and ice ages. They discovered optimism in men's most ancient teachers. 'The hard thing gives way' is the maxim which Brecht's customs official elicits from the Chinese sage in the poem 'Legend of the Origin of the Book Tao Te Ching on Lao Tzu's Way into Exile'. And Benjamin comments: 'The poem comes to us at a time when such words ring in the ears of men like a promise which has nothing to concede to the promises of a Messiah. For the contemporary reader, however, they contain not only a promise but a lesson:

"... That yielding water in motion
Gets the better in the end of granite and porphyry."'

To align oneself with all those things which, like water, are 'inconspicuous and sober and inexhaustible' would remind one, Benjamin argued, of the cause of the losers and the oppressed. In his 'Sixth Thesis on the Philosophy of History' (in *Illuminations*), he wrote: 'Only the historian will have the gift of fanning the spark of hope in the past who is firmly convinced that *even the dead* will not be safe from the enemy if he wins. And this enemy has not ceased to be victorious.' History was for him an ever-present arena, never (as with Lukács) merely the 'preconditions of the present'. The battles of the past had to be fought and refought; if not they might be lost again.

Benjamin puts this thesis into practice in his analysis of Brecht's Lao Tzu poem. Here the 'spark of hope in the past' is that momentary 'friendship' between sage and customs official which elicits Lao Tzu's wisdom. Such friendliness forms Brecht's and Benjamin's 'minimum programme of humanity'; and Benjamin concludes his commentary with the sage-like injunction: 'Whoever wants to make the hard thing give way should miss no opportunity for friendliness.'

At the end of the 'Conversations', Benjamin quotes a Brechtian maxim: 'Don't start from the good old things but the bad new ones.' The same phrase occurs in a Brecht essay on Lukács, whom he criticizes for a lingering attachment to the old masters and the 'good old days' of bourgeois culture. Lukács opposes the patrician Thomas Mann to Kafka, insecure visionary of despair. In the 'Conversations' Benjamin and Brecht tussle over Kafka. Brecht accuses Benjamin of prolonging Kafka's own self-mystifications. Yet elsewhere Brecht was to include Kafka among those 'documents of despair' from which Socialist writers may learn because of their innovating literary techniques.

What is 'bad' about Kafka is the despair; what is 'new' is not merely the technique, but the kinds of perception and understanding that inform it. Brecht describes Kafka's outlook as that of 'a man caught under the wheels', of the petty bourgeois who is 'bound to get it in the neck'. But this is not the petty bourgeois who turns to fascism, to a leader. Even from under the wheels he continues to ask questions; 'he is wise'. It is, as Benjamin says of Brecht's Galy Gay in *A Man's a Man*, the wisdom of a man 'who lets the contradictions of existence enter into the only place where they can, in the last analysis, be resolved: the life of a man'. Kafka's heroes are crushed under the wheels. Nevertheless, they number, along with Schweyk and Leopold Bloom, among the potential 'wise men' of the 'bad new' days. It is with them, victims and flotsam of mass society, that Brecht begins. Where Lukács had berated twentieth-century literature for not producing 'rounded characters', Brecht rejoined that dehumanization would not be lifted by leaving the mass, but by becoming part of it. In his hands, the Kafkaesque victim, the anonymous K., the petty bourgeois under the wheels, becomes the Brechtian K., the canny Herr Keuner. Similarly, Benjamin remarks of Galy Gay: 'A man's a man: this is not fidelity to any single essence of one's own, but a continual readiness to admit a new essence.' The 'bad new' days destroy personality, create anonymity. Brecht and Benjamin start with the anonymous man and encourage his resilience, so that the 'hard thing' may give way. But because of their fear of a new dark age, they think in a perspective which goes beyond the immediate class struggle to encompass all the social struggles of humanity, where qualities like cunning and endurance are more important than heroism. Brecht's drama and poetry form a humanist *vademecum* for dark ages. His 'heroes' are resourceful, humorous nobodies.

Epic Theatre

Epic theatre is the product of a *historical* imagination. Brecht's 'plagiarism', his rewriting of Shakespeare and Marlowe, are experiments in whether a historical event and its literary treatment might be made to turn out differently or at least be viewed differently, if the processes of history are revalued. Brecht's drama is a deliberate unseating of the supremacy of tragedy and tragic inevitability. His 'historical pessimism' cuts the ground from under the truly pessimistic 'optimism' of all those who place their faith in historical inevitability. Echoing his own 'Theses on the Philosophy of History', Benjamin comments: ' "It can happen this way, but it can also happen quite a different way" – that is the fundamental attitude of one who writes for epic theatre.' The possibility that history might have been different will inspire a *tua res agitur* in the minds of present-day spectators: history may now be different; it is in your hands, even though the means at your disposal are slight and the qualities required of you are perhaps undramatic, unromantic. Hence, in recovering the past, the epic dramatist will 'tend to emphasize not the great decisions which lie along the main line of history but the incommensurable and the singular'.

Benjamin's encounter with Brecht leads him, in 'What is Epic Theatre?' (of which the two existing versions are given here), to sketch out a new theory of the history of drama which is already suggested in his earlier, pre-Marxist *Ursprung des deutschen Trauer-spiels*. Benjamin saw affinity between the allegoric imagination of the German baroque dramatists and the artistic needs of the twentieth century; first in the melancholy spirit of the former, with its emblematic but inscrutable insignia, which he rediscovered in Kafka; then in the cognate principle of montage which he found in the work of Eisenstein and Brecht. Montage became for him the modern, constructive, active, unmelancholy form of allegory, namely the ability to connect dissimilars in such a way as to 'shock' people into new recognitions and understandings. A great deal of Benjamin's critical writing concerns itself with 'shock' as the primary experience of dislocation in modern urban, mass, industrial life. He considered Baudelaire and Proust, for example, sensitive reactors to the new 'shocks' of modern life, who at the same time used their art as a means of self-protection. Such self-protection, he argued, is no longer needed by the revolutionary artist who welcomes 'shock' with critical distance, with 'heightened presence of mind'. Thus Benjamin came to regard montage, i.e. the ability to capture the infinite, sudden or subterranean connections of dissimilars, as the major constitutive principle of the artistic imagination in the age of technology.

For fruitful antecedents, he looks back beyond German baroque to those forms of drama where the montage principle first made its appearance. He finds it wherever a critical intelligence intervenes to comment upon the representation, in other words where the representation is never complete in itself, but is openly and continually compared with the life represented; where the actors can at any moment stand outside themselves and show themselves to be actors.

Once more Chinese culture plays its part in the thinking of the two men. Benjamin points to the custom of Chinese theatre to 'make what is shown on the stage unsensational' and underlines Brecht's debt to this technique. Then, very originally, he sketches out a byway of European theatre which, he suggests, had always sought to escape from the 'closed' drama of Greek tragedy, had always sought for an untragic drama. The untragic drama and the montage principle were closely connected in Benjamin's mind. That byway led via the medieval mystery play, German baroque drama, certain scenes of Shakespeare, Part II of Goethe's *Faust*, to Strindberg and finally Brecht and 'epic theatre': 'If, that is, one can speak of a path at all, rather than an overgrown stalking-track along which the legacy of medieval and baroque drama has crept down to us over the sublime but barren massif of classicism.'

Benjamin quotes from the early Lukács to found a theory which takes an entirely opposed direction to Lukács's own subsequent dramaturgy. The later Lukács, concerned with the 'main line of history', treated 'stalking-tracks' as either non-existent or unworthy of mention. Basing himself on Hegel's concept of tragedy, he categorized the dramatic hero as an exponent of will, the protagonist of a conflict between two mutually exclusive ethical demands. To carry through his will against all obstacles was the hero's sole aim, his glory and his defeat. Benjamin, however, noted: 'Plato, Lukács wrote twenty years ago, already recognized the undramatic nature of the highest form of man, the sage. And yet in his dialogues he brought him to the threshold of the stage.' That is, with Plato begins Benjamin's alternative history of European drama, where the wise and dispassionate man is hero. Indeed, Socrates applauded the new 'rationalist' drama of Euripides, which concluded the great period of Greek tragedy. And Benjamin considered Brecht a 'Socratic' dramatist: 'One may regard epic theatre as more dramatic than the dialogue (it is not always): but epic theatre need not, for that reason, be any the less philosophical.'

In Brecht's transformation, the sage, from Galy Gay in *A Man's a Man* to Azdak in the *Caucasian Chalk Circle* and Matti in *Herr Puntila*, is the man who has suffered and travelled much, who changes his role to suit his circumstances. He is, in Benjamin's words, 'an empty stage on which the contradictions of our society are acted out'. It is through this 'empty', 'consenting', pliant, adaptable 'hero' that some of the principles of montage – *Verfremdung* (alienation), exchanging roles and identities – may best be enacted. Such a device is used by Eliot in *The Waste Land*, in the figure of the hermaphrodite blind seer, Tiresias, who has seen everything before, who witnesses and suffers everything again. But he is a figure of nostalgia, a traditional stoic sage who speaks the language of snobbish irony and can bequeath nothing to posterity but the primal syllables of the Indo-European tongue. Brecht's sages or 'thinking men' are by contrast men of sense and vitality. Galy Gay learns his lesson, masters his situation, and for all his adaptability, indeed because of it, proves the only humane person in the play; able to show 'friendliness' to the man whose identity he allowed himself to rob. Azdak, the rogue, can make justice reign for a brief talismanic hour. Galileo, though not a man of the people, but who belongs with the 'adaptable' heroes, can, in the second version of the play, which Benjamin did not live to read, make a self-critique of the scientist that encompasses the history of professional men from the Renaissance to the present.

In his metaphysically probing thought, Benjamin sees Brecht's epic theatre as a form not merely of 'Socratic', but of truly Platonic drama. The aim of the address, 'The Author as Producer', is to find a political answer, a political rôle for the artist that would placate Plato's strictures in the *Republic*. Benjamin's historical imagination uncovers a path that leads from the dialogues to epic theatre. In his disquisitions on Brecht, Benjamin seeks to rescue the artist in Plato, whom Plato himself feared.

Art and Politics

In one respect, by eliding the politicization of art with the use of artistic 'means of production' or apparatus, Benjamin and Brecht at times constricted the relationship between politics and art. Brecht, in his later theory and practice, was able to clarify this confusion. Benjamin died before he could completely think through a new materialist aesthetics.

Brecht's earlier attitudes were shaped by Piscator and the Russian ex-Futurists, like Tretyakov, for whom the destruction of a theatre of illusion meant a frontal attack on the bourgeoisie itself. Stanislavskian reproduction was considered bourgeois as such. To be anti-bourgeois or proletarian was to show how things worked, while they were being shown; to 'lay bare the device' (in the words of the

Russian Formalists). Art should be considered a form of production, not a mystery; the stage should appear like a factory with the machinery fully exposed.

Certainly the Doric or Corinthian pillars which fronted the bourgeois bank served a reactionary purpose. But the modern glass-plated banks show nothing more of the workings of capitalism. As an analogy with Brechtian theory, this would be crude and unfair, for, as we have seen, it was precisely the use of montage which constructed the political connections that were not immediately visible. Nevertheless, throughout the left-wing avant-garde art of the twenties and thirties, the belief predominated that to attack and repudiate 'illusionism' or 'reproduction' itself constituted a progressive political act, constituted *the* way in which politics could enter directly into art. This belief continues to affect all radical and left thinking on aesthetics today.

Benjamin's development up to this point had been singular. He began, very typically for the time, as an aesthetic philosopher who lamented the passing of old traditions, as modern technology and mass society took their place. He was anything but a revolutionary avant-garde thinker. He was always avant-garde, but in the spirit of an Eliot (with whom indeed he shared a great deal: Eliot's recovery of the metaphysical poets stems from the same roots as Benjamin's interest in German baroque drama), and as a critic he matched the associative, allegorical powers of Eliot's poetry.

Benjamin's attitude to the newspaper illustrates his further evolution. In 'The Storyteller', his essay on Leskov in *Illuminations*, Benjamin contrasts the self-preserving, self-containing powers of the story, that most ancient bearer of wisdom, with the mere giving-out of information that is *par excellence* the role of the newspaper.

In 'The Author as Producer' (paradoxically, probably composed earlier than 'The Storyteller') a change of enormous scale is evident in his thinking. The newspaper, or at least the contemporary Soviet newspaper, Benjamin here describes as a 'vast melting-down process' which 'not only destroys the conventional separation between genres, between writer and poet, scholar and popularizer' but 'questions even the separation between author and reader'. The 'place where the word is most debased – that is to say, the newspaper – becomes the very place where a rescue operation can be mounted'.

The Chinese wall newspaper of the Cultural Revolution, the posters, inscriptions and roneoed sheets of the Parisian (and other) students in 1968, all bear Benjamin out and make this once melancholy, metaphysical *littérateur* into the foremost revolutionary and radical critic of the nineteen-sixties and seventies. The spread of street-theatre, agitprop, 'interaction' likewise vindicate Benjamin's and Brecht's views of the theatre. At the same time their enthusiasm and radicalism conceal a potentially harmful one-sidedness. Thus the very democratization of art by means of the media of reproduction is used to oust and reject all traditional forms of art associated with a division of performer and audience, owner and onlooker. Benjamin simply identifies 'aura', the aesthetic nimbus surrounding a work of art, with property, and mechanical reproduction with proletarianization. Of course, mechanical reproduction can be and is abused and absorbed by capitalism, and Benjamin was an early, perceptive diagnostician of this danger. As a preventive (or, if necessary, a cure) he argued for the social control of the media. In this there was nothing new. What was challenging was the suggestion that such social control would create new forms of art; more, that the politicization of the media was the same as the politicization of art. In other words, media and art were identified. The old distinction between form and content was abolished; form itself became political.

By thus collapsing content into form, the range of forms may be restricted. Because Benjamin was the child of the first phase of a new technological era, when techniques like photo-montage had a direct political effect, he sometimes tended to isolate technique as politically effective in itself and to ignore that the politicization of technology involves the relations, as well as the means, of production.

At the same time as he championed the 'bad new things', Benjamin's philosophy of history, as we have seen, required a constant battle on behalf of the past, on behalf of its victims. He sought to solve this contradiction with the concept of *Jetztzeit*, ('the presence of the now'), a *nunc stans*, in which time stands still, where past and future converge not harmoniously, but explosively, in the present instant.

This concept of *Jetztzeit*, together with that of *Ermattungstaktik* ('tactics of attrition'), were the two ideas or predispositions that dominated Benjamin's thinking during his last years. *Jetztzeit* entailed the ability to intervene in events, whether as politician or intellectual, to 'blast open the continuum of history' (Sixteenth Thesis on the Philosophy of History). The idea is important in view of the progressivist, evolutionist, determinist traditions of Social Democracy on the one hand, which Benjamin explicitly attacked in his 'Theses on the Philosophy of History'; and the 'Utopian' positivism and pragmatism of the Soviet Union under Stalin on the other. In linking the idea of *Jetztzeit* with the Socialist revolutionary movement Benjamin joins ranks with Gramsci and the Lukács of *History and Class Consciousness* (one of the Marxist texts which most influenced him).

The other idea or attitude, *Ermattungstaktik*, Brecht described in a poem full of pessimism written after Benjamin's death.

> *Ermattungstaktik war's, was dir behagte*
> *Am Schachtisch sitzend in des Birnbaums Schatten.*
> *Der Feind, der dich von deinen Büchern jagte*
> *Lässt sich von unsereinem nicht ermatten.*

> [Tactics of attrition are what you enjoyed
> Sitting at the chess table in the pear tree's shade.
> The enemy who drove you from your books
> Will not be worn down by the likes of us.]

The philosophy of *Ermattung* dominates Benjamin's writings on Brecht, the belief that in the end 'the hard thing gives way'. The dialectical essence of Benjamin's thought lies in the polarity of *Jetztzeit* and *Ermattung*; the 'Messianic' intervention in, and control over, history (however small the proportions and shortlived the duration), the expectation, expressed in the last 'Thesis on the Philosophy of History', that 'every second of time was the straight gate through which the Messiah might come', and the sober, sage-like, patient wearing down of hardness. It was this sense of expectation that Benjamin's friend and contemporary Ernst Bloch translated into the category of 'concrete Utopia' or the ontological principle of hope.

Bloch wrote of Benjamin's suicide that it was 'a kind of parting with life not so uncharacteristic of him, if one thinks of a phrase of his which I recall: "Least of all has one power over a dead man"'. In a similar vein Brecht wrote in a second poem on his friend's death:

> *Zuletzt an eine unüberschreitbare Grenze getrieben*
> *Hast du, heisst es, eine überschreitbare überschritten*
> [In the end driven to an impassable frontier
> You, we hear, passed over a passable one.]

Benjamin committed suicide at Port Bou on the Franco-Spanish frontier, in September 1940, on hearing that he was likely to be handed over to the Gestapo the following day. Brecht remarked, when he received the news of his death, that this was the first real loss that Hitler had caused to German literature.

STANLEY MITCHELL
London, 1972

WHAT IS EPIC THEATRE?* [FIRST VERSION]

The point at issue in the theatre today can be more accurately defined in relation to the stage than to the play. It concerns the filling-in of the orchestra pit. The abyss which separates the actors from the audience like the dead from the living, the abyss whose silence heightens the sublime in drama, whose resonance heightens the intoxication of opera, this abyss which, of all the elements of the stage, most indelibly bears the traces of its sacral origins, has lost its function. The stage is still elevated, but it no longer rises from an immeasurable depth; it has become a public platform. Upon this platform the theatre now has to install itself. That is the situation. But, as happens in many situations, here too the business of disguising it has prevailed over its proper realization. Tragedies and operas go on and on being written, apparently with a trusty stage apparatus to hand, whereas in reality they do nothing but supply material for an apparatus which is obsolete. 'This confusion among musicians, writers and critics about their situation has enormous consequences which receive far too little attention. Believing themselves to be in possession of an apparatus which in

---

* Bibliographical details of where these essays were first published are given on page 123.

reality possesses them, they defend an apparatus over which they no longer have control, which is no longer, as they still believe, a means *for* the producers but has become a means to be used against the producers.' With these words Brecht dispels the illusion that theatre today is based on literature. That is true neither for the commercial theatre nor for his own. In both, the text is the servant: in the former it serves to keep the business going, in the latter to change it. How is such change possible? Is there such a thing as drama for the public platform – for that is what the stage has become – or, as Brecht says, for 'public propaganda institutes'? And if so, what is its nature? The only possibility of doing justice to the public platform appeared to have been found by the 'theatre of current events', the *Zeittheater*, in the form of political plays. But however this political theatre functioned, socially it promoted the occupation by the proletarian masses of the very positions which the apparatus of the theatre had created for the bourgeois masses. The functional relationship between stage and public, text and performance, producer and actors, remained almost unchanged. Epic theatre takes as its starting point the attempt to introduce fundamental change into these relationships. For its public, the stage is no longer 'the planks which signify the world' (in other words, a magic circle), but a convenient public exhibition area. For its stage, the public is no longer a collection of hypnotized test subjects, but an assembly of interested persons whose demands it must satisfy. For its text, the performance is no longer a virtuoso interpretation, but its rigorous control. For its performance, the text is no longer a basis of that performance, but a grid on which, in the form of new formulations, the gains of that performance are marked. For its actor, the producer no longer gives him instructions about effects, but theses for comment. For its producer, the actor is no longer a mime who must embody a role, but a functionary who has to make an inventory of it.

Clearly, functions thus changed must be founded on changed elements. A recent (1931) Berlin performance of Brecht's parable *A Man's a Man* offered the best opportunity to test this. Thanks to the courageous and intelligent assiduity of Legal, the theatre director, this was not only one of the most precisely studied productions seen in Berlin for years; it was also a model of epic theatre, the only one so far. What prevented the professional critics from recognizing this fact will be seen in due course. The public found Brecht's comedy perfectly accessible – once the sultry atmosphere of the first night had cleared – without help from any professional criticism. For the difficulties encountered by epic theatre in achieving recognition are, after all, nothing other than an expression of its closeness to real life, while theory languishes in the Babylonian exile of a praxis which has nothing to do with the way we live. Thus, the values of an operetta by Kolla lend themselves more readily to definition in the approved language of aesthetics than those of a play by Brecht, especially since such a play, in order totally to dedicate itself to the construction of the new theatre, allows itself a free hand with literature.

Epic theatre is gestural. The extent to which it can also be literary in the traditional sense is a separate issue. The gesture is its raw material and its task is the rational utilization of this material. The gesture has two advantages over the highly deceptive statements and assertions normally made by people and their many-layered and opaque actions. First, the gesture is falsifiable only up to a point; in fact, the more inconspicuous and habitual it is, the more difficult it is to falsify. Second, unlike people's actions and endeavours, it has a definable beginning and a definable end. Indeed, this strict, frame-like, enclosed nature of each moment of an attitude which, after all, is as a whole in a state of living flux, is one of the basic dialectical characteristics of the gesture. This leads to an important conclusion: the more frequently we interrupt someone engaged in an action, the more gestures we obtain. Hence, the interrupting of action is one of the principal concerns of epic theatre. Therein lies the formal achievement of Brecht's songs with their crude, heart-rending refrains. Without anticipating the difficult study, yet to be made, of the function of the text in epic theatre, we can at least say that often its main function is not to illustrate or advance the action but, on the contrary, to interrupt it: not only the action of others, but also the action of one's own. It is the retarding quality of these interruptions and the episodic quality of this framing of action which allows gestural theatre to become epic theatre.

The job of epic theatre, it has been explained, is not so much to develop actions as to represent conditions. Most of the slogans of the dramaturgy of epic theatre have been ignored but this one has, at least, created a misunderstanding. Reason enough to take it up. Those 'conditions' which had to be represented were thought to be the equivalent of the 'milieu', or social setting, of earlier theoreticians. Thus understood, the demand meant no more than a plea for a return to naturalistic drama. Yet no one can be naive enough to champion such a return. The naturalistic stage is in no sense a public platform; it is entirely illusionistic. Its own awareness that it is theatre cannot fertilize it; like every theatre of unfolding action, it must repress this awareness so as to pursue undistracted its aim of portraying the real. Epic theatre, by contrast, incessantly derives a lively and productive consciousness from the fact that it is theatre. This consciousness enables it to treat elements of reality as though it were setting up an experiment, with the 'conditions' at the end of the experiment, not at the beginning. Thus they are not brought closer to the spectator but distanced from him. When he recognizes them as real conditions it is not, as in naturalistic theatre, with complacency, but with astonishment. This astonishment is the means whereby epic theatre, in a hard, pure way, revives a Socratic praxis. In one who is astonished, interest is born: interest in its primordial form. Nothing is more characteristic of Brecht's way of thinking than the attempt which epic theatre makes to transform this primordial interest directly into a technical, expert one. Epic theatre addresses itself to interested persons 'who do not think unless they have a reason to'. But that is an attitude absolutely shared by the masses. Brecht's dialectical materialism asserts itself unmistakably in his endeavour to interest the masses in theatre as technical experts, but not at all by way of 'culture'. 'In this way we could very soon have a theatre full of experts, as we have sports stadiums full of experts.'

Epic theatre, then, does not reproduce conditions but, rather, reveals them. This uncovering of conditions is brought about through processes being interrupted. A very crude example: a family row. The mother is just about to pick up a pillow to hurl at the daughter, the father is opening a window to call a policeman. At this moment a stranger appears at the door. 'Tableau', as they used to say around 1900. In other words: the stranger is suddenly confronted with certain conditions: rumpled bedclothes, open window, a devastated interior. But there exists a view in which even the more usual scenes of bourgeois life appear rather like this. The more far-reaching the devastations of our social order (the more these devastations undermine ourselves and out capacity to remain aware of them), the more marked must be the distance between the stranger and the events portrayed. We know such a stranger from Brecht's *Versuche*: a Swabian 'Utis', a counterpart of Ulysses, the Greek 'Nobody' who visits one-eyed Polyphemus in his cave. Similarly Keuner – that is the stranger's name – penetrates into the cave of the one-eyed monster whose name is 'class society'. Like Ulysses he is full of guile, accustomed to suffering, much-travelled; both men are wise. A practical resignation which has always shunned utopian idealism makes Ulysses think only of returning home; Keuner never leaves the threshold of his house at all. He likes the trees which he sees in the yard when he comes out of his fourth-floor tenement flat. 'Why don't you ever go into the woods,' ask his friends, 'if you like trees so much?' 'Did I not tell you,' replies Herr Keuner, 'that I like the trees in my yard?' To move this thinking man, Herr Keuner (who, Brecht once suggested, should be carried on stage lying down, so little is he drawn thither), to move him to existence upon the stage – that is the aim of this new theatre. It will be noticed, not without surprise, that its origins reach back a very long time. For the fact is that ever since the Greeks, the search for the untragic hero on the European stage has never ceased. Despite all the classical revivals, the great dramatists have always kept as far away as possible from the authentic Greek figure of tragedy. This is not the place to trace the path which winds through the Middle Ages, in Hroswitha and the mystery plays, or later, in Gryphius, Lenz and Grabbe, or to show how Goethe crossed it in the second *Faust*. But we may say that this path was a specially German one. If, that is, one can speak of a path at all, rather than an overgrown stalking-track along which the legacy of medieval and baroque drama has crept down to us over the sublime but barren massif of classicism. This track reappears today, rough and untended as it may be, in the plays of Brecht. The untragic hero is part of this German tradition. That his paradoxical stage existence has to be redeemed by our own actual one was recognized at an early date; not, of course, by the critics, but by the best contemporary thinkers such as Georg Lukács and Franz Rosenzweig. Plato, Lukács wrote twenty years ago, already recognized the undramatic nature of the highest form of man, the sage. And yet in his dialogues he brought him to the threshold of the stage. One may regard epic theatre as more dramatic than the dialogue (it is not always): but epic theatre need not, for that reason, be any the less philosophical.

The forms of epic theatre correspond to the new technical forms – cinema and radio. Epic theatre corresponds to the modern level of technology. In film, the theory has become more and more accepted that the audience should be able to 'come in' at any point, that complicated plot developments should be avoided and that each part, besides the value it has for the whole, should also possess its own episodic value. For radio, with its public which can freely switch on or off at any moment, this becomes a strict necessity. Epic theatre introduces the same practice on the stage. For epic theatre, as a matter of principle, there is no such thing as a latecomer. The implications of this suggest that epic theatre's challenge to the theatre as a social institution is far more serious than any damage it may inflict on the theatre as entertainment industry. Whereas, in cabaret, the bourgeoisie mingle with bohemia and, in variety, the gap between petty and big bourgeoisie is bridged for the space of an evening, the habitués of Brecht's theatre, where cigarette smoke is caught in the projector beam, are proletarians. For them there is nothing strange about Brecht's instruction to an actor to play the choosing of a wooden leg by the beggar in the *Threepenny Opera* in such a way that 'just for the sake of seeing this particular turn people will plan to revisit the show at the precise moment it occurs'. Neher's back-projections for such 'turns' are far more like posters than stage decorations. The poster is a constituent element of 'literarized' theatre. 'Literarizing entails punctuating "representation" with "formulation"; gives the theatre the possibility of making contact with other institutions for intellectual activities.'* These institutions (media) even include books. 'Footnotes, and the habit of turning back in order to check a point, need to be introduced into playwriting too.'

But what is it that Neher's posters advertise? Brecht writes that they 'adopt an attitude towards events in such a way that the real glutton in Mahagonny sits in front of the depicted glutton'. Very well. Who can say that the acted glutton is more real than the depicted one? We can make the acted one sit in front of the more real one, i.e. we can let the depicted one at the back be more real than the acted one. Perhaps it is only now that we obtain a clue to the powerful and curious effect of scenes staged in this way. Some of the players appear as mandatories of the larger forces which, remaining in the background, are like Plato's Ideas in that they constitute the ideal model of things. Neher's back-projections, however, are materialist ideas; they relate to genuine 'conditions'; even when they approximate to actual events, the tremulousness of their contours still suggests the far greater and more intimate proximity from which they have been wrenched in order to become visible.

The literarization of theatre by means of verbal formulas, posters, captions, is intended to, and will, 'make what is shown on the stage unsensational'. (Brecht is fully aware of the connections between these methods and certain practices of Chinese theatre, a connection which we will examine at some future date.) Brecht goes still further in the same direction by asking himself whether the events portrayed by the epic actor ought not to be known in advance. 'In that case historical events would, on the face of it, be the most suitable.' One must, however, expect the dramatist to take a certain amount of licence in that he will tend to emphasize not the great decisions

* *Brecht on Theatre: The Development of an Aesthetic*, edited and translated by John Willett, Hill and Wang, New York, 1964, pp. 43–4 (Translator's note).

which lie along the main line of history but the incommensurable and the singular. 'It can happen this way, but it can also happen quite a different way' – that is the fundamental attitude of one who writes for epic theatre. His relation to his story is like that of a ballet teacher to his pupil. His first aim is to loosen her joints to the very limits of the possible. He will be as far removed from historical and psychological clichés as Strindberg in his historical dramas. For Strindberg made a strongly conscious attempt at epic, untragic theatre. In the works concerned with individual lives he still goes back to the Christian schema of the Passion; but in his histories the vehemence of his critical thought and his irony with its unmasking effect pave the way for epic theatre. In this sense, the Calvary play *To Damascus* and the morality play *Gustavus Adolphus* are the twin poles of his dramatic writing.

If we adopt the optic which we have just outlined, we can see the productive dichotomy between Brecht and the so-called *Zeit-dramatik*, a dichotomy which he tries to overcome in his *Lehr-stücke* (didactic plays). These plays are the necessary detour via epic theatre which the play with a thesis must take. The plays of a Toller or a Lampel do not take this detour; exactly like the works of German pseudo-classicism, they 'award primacy to the idea, and all the time make the spectator desire a specific aim, creating, as it were, an ever-increasing demand for the supply'. Such writers attack the conditions in which we live from the outside; Brecht lets the conditions speak for themselves, so that they confront each other dialectically. Their various elements are played off logically against one another. The docker Galy Gay in Brecht's *A Man's a Man* is like an empty stage on which the contradictions of our society are acted out. Following Brecht's line of thought one might arrive at the proposition that it is the wise man who is the perfect stage for such a dialectic. In any case Galy Gay is a wise man. He introduces himself as a docker 'who doesn't drink, smokes very little and hasn't any passions to speak of'. He is not tempted by the offer of sex with the widow whose basket he has carried. 'To be frank, I'd really like to buy some fish.' Yet he is introduced as a man 'who can't say no'. And this too is wise, for he lets the contradictions of existence enter into the only place where they can, in the last analysis, be resolved: the life of a man. Only the 'consenting' man has any chance of changing the world.

And so it happens that the wise proletarian Galy Gay, the man who keeps himself to himself, agrees to join the berserk ranks of the British colonial army, thereby consenting to the denial of his own wisdom. A moment ago he went out of his front door, sent by his wife on an errand to buy some fish. Now he meets three soldiers of the Anglo-Indian army who have lost a fourth while looting a pagoda. The three of them have their own reasons for finding a replacement for the missing man as soon as possible. Galy Gay is the man who can't say no. He follows the three soldiers without knowing what is in store for him. One by one he adopts thoughts, attitudes, habits such as a soldier in war must possess; when he is completely re-equipped, he won't even recognize his own wife when she eventually succeeds in tracking him down. Finally he becomes the much-feared conqueror of the Tibetan mountain stronghold of So al Dohowr. A man's a man, so a docker is a mercenary. He will treat his self-condition as mercenary no differently from the way he treated his dockerhood. A man's a man: this is not fidelity to any single essence of one's own, but a continual readiness to admit a new essence.

> Never give your exact name, what's the point?
> When you name yourself you always name another.
> Don't be so loud in stating your opinion. Forget it. What
>   was it again, the opinion you held?
> Do not remember things for longer than they last.

Epic theatre casts doubts upon the notion that theatre is entertainment. It shakes the social validity of theatre-as-entertainment by robbing it of its function within the capitalist system. It also threatens the privileges of the critics. These privileges are based on the technical expertise which enables the critic to make certain observations about productions and performances. The criteria he applies in making his observations are only very rarely within his own control; he seldom worries about this, but relies upon 'theatre aesthetics' in the details of which nobody is particularly interested. If, however, the aesthetic of the theatre ceases to remain in the background, if its forum is the audience and its criterion is no longer the effect registered by the nervous systems of single individuals but the degree to which the mass of spectators becomes a coherent whole, then the critic as he is constituted today is no longer ahead of that mass but actually finds himself far behind it. The moment when the mass begins to differentiate itself in discussion and responsible decisions, or in attempts to discover well-founded attitudes of its own, the moment the false and deceptive totality called 'audience' begins to disintegrate and there is new space for the formation of separate parties within it – separate parties corresponding to conditions as they really are – at that moment the critic suffers the double misfortune of seeing his nature as agent revealed and, at the same time, devalued. Simply by the fact of appealing to an 'audience' – which continues to exist in its old, opaque form only for the theatre, but characteristically, no longer for film – the critic becomes, whether he means to or not, the advocate of what the ancients used to call 'theatrocratia': the use of theatre to dominate the masses by manipulating their reflexes and sensations – the exact opposite of responsible collectives freely choosing their positions. The 'innovations' which such audiences will demand are exclusively concerned with what is realizable within existing society, and are thus the opposite of 'renovations'. Epic theatre attacks the basic view that art may do no more than lightly touch upon experience – the view which grants only to kitsch the right to encompass the whole range of experience, and then only for the lower classes of society. This attack upon the basis is at the same time an assault upon the critics' privileges. And this the critics have sensed; in the debate over epic theatre they must be considered an interested party.

Naturally, such 'self-control' of the stage counts on there being actors whose idea of the audience is essentially different from the animal-tamer's view of the beasts who inhabit his cage: actors for whom effect is not an end but a means. The Russian producer Meyerhold was recently asked in Berlin what in his opinion distinguished his actors from those of Western Europe. He replied:

'Two things. First, they think; second, they do not think idealistic-ally but materialistically.' The view that the stage is a moral insti-tution is justified only in relation to a theatre that does not merely transmit knowledge but actually engenders it. In epic theatre the actor's training consists in acting in such a way that he is oriented towards knowledge; and this knowledge, in turn, determines not only the content but also the *tempi*, pauses and stresses of his whole per-formance. This should not, however, be understood in the sense of a style. In the programme notes to *A Man's a Man* we read: 'In epic theatre the actor has several functions, and according to the particular function he is fulfilling, the style of his acting will change.' This plurality of possibilities is controlled by a dialectic to which all stylistic considerations have to bow. 'The actor must show an event, and he must show himself. He naturally shows the event by showing himself, and he shows himself by showing the event. Al-though these two tasks coincide, they must not coincide to such a point that the contrast (difference) between them disappears.'

'To make gestures quotable' is the actor's most important achieve-ment; he must be able to space his gestures as the compositor pro-duces spaced type. 'The epic play is a construction that must be viewed rationally and in which things must be recognized; therefore the way it is presented must go half-way to meet such viewing.' The supreme task of an epic production is to give expression to the rela-tionship between the action being staged and everything that is in-volved in the act of staging *per se*. The general educational approach of Marxism is determined by the dialectic at work between the atti-tude of teaching and that of learning: something similar occurs in epic theatre with the constant dialectic between the action which is shown on the stage and the attitude of showing an action on the stage. The first commandment of epic theatre is that 'the one who shows' – that is, the actor – 'shall be shown'. Some will perhaps find that such a formulation is reminiscent of Tieck's old 'dramaturgy of reflexion'. To show why this view is mistaken would be to con-struct a spiral staircase to climb to the rigging-loft of Brechtian theory. It should suffice here to make just one point: for all its skills of reflexion, the Romantic stage never succeeded in doing justice to the fundamental dialectical relationship between theory and praxis; its struggle to achieve this was, in its way, as vain as that of the *Zeittheater* today.

If, then, the actor on the old stage sometimes found himself, as 'comedian', rubbing shoulders with the priest, in epic theatre he finds himself beside the philosopher. His gesture demonstrates the social significance and applicability of dialectics. It tests conditions on men. The difficulties which a producer meets in rehearsing a play cannot be resolved without concrete understanding of the body of society. But the dialectic which epic theatre sets out to present is not dependent on a sequence of scenes in time; rather, it declares itself in those gestural elements that form the basis of each sequence in time. (These gestural elements are not elemental in the strict sense of the word but only inasmuch as they are simpler than the sequences based upon them.) The thing that is revealed as though by lightning in the 'condition' represented on the stage – as a copy of human gestures, actions and words – is an immanently dialectical attitude. The conditions which epic theatre reveals is the dialectic at a standstill. For just as, in Hegel, the sequence of time is not the mother of the dialectic but only the medium in which the dialectic manifests itself, so in epic theatre the dialectic is not born of the contradiction between successive statements or ways of behaving, but of the gesture itself.

Twice Galy Gay is summoned to a wall, the first time to change his clothes, the second time to be shot; in both cases the summoning gesture is the same. He himself uses another gesture twice: the first time to renounce the fish he wanted to buy, the second time to accept the elephant. This is the kind of discovery that will satisfy the interest of the audience who frequent epic theatre; it is with discoveries like these that they will get their money's worth. The author, when discussing what distinguishes the epic theatre from the ordinary theatre of entertainment as a more serious art form, is right to point out: 'When we call the other theatre, the one that is hostile to us, merely culinary we create the impression that in our theatre we are against all fun, as though we could not imagine learning or being taught other than as an intensely unpleasurable process. One is often obliged to weaken one's own position in order to fight an opponent, and to rob one's cause of its breadth and validity for the sake of immediate advantage. Thus reduced purely to fighting form, the cause may win, but it cannot replace what it has defeated. Yet the act of recognizing of which we speak is itself a pleasurable act. The simple fact that man can be recognized in a certain way creates a sense of triumph, and the fact, too, that he can never be recognized completely, never once and for all, that he is not so easily exhaustible, that he holds and conceals so many possibilities within himself (hence his capacity for development), is a pleasurable recognition. That man can be changed by his surroundings and can himself change the surrounding world, i.e. can treat it with consequence, all this produces feelings of pleasure. Not, of course, if man is viewed as something mechanical, something that can be put into a slot, something lacking resistance, as happens today under the weight of certain social conditions. Astonishment, which must here be inserted into the Aristotelian formula for the effects of tragedy, should be considered entirely as a capacity. It can be learned.'

The damming of the stream of real life, the moment when its flow comes to a standstill, makes itself felt as reflux: this reflux is astonishment. The dialectic at a standstill is its real object. It is the rock from which we gaze down into that stream of things which, in the city of Jehoo 'that's always full and where nobody stays', they have a song about:

> Rest not on the wave which breaks against your foot,
> So long as it stands in the water, new waves will break against it.

But if the stream of things breaks against this rock of astonishment, then there is no difference between a human life and a word. In epic theatre both are only the crest of the wave. Epic theatre makes life spurt up high from the bed of time and, for an instant, hover iridescent in empty space. Then it puts it back to bed.

WHAT IS EPIC THEATRE? [SECOND VERSION]

I   *The Relaxed Audience*

'Nothing is more pleasant than to lie on a sofa reading a novel', wrote one of the epic authors of the last century. The remark suggests the degree of relaxation which a narrative work can give to its reader. If we imagine a person attending a dramatic spectacle we tend to visualize the opposite. We see someone who, with every fibre of his being, is intently following a process. The concept of epic theatre (developed by Brecht, the theoretician of his own poetic praxis) implies, above all, that the audience which this theatre desires to attract is a relaxed one, following the play in a relaxed manner. True, such an audience will always occur as a collective, unlike the reader of a novel alone with his text. Furthermore, in most cases this audience – again, as a collective – will quickly feel impelled to take up an attitude towards what it sees. But this attitude, Brecht thinks, should be a considered and therefore a relaxed one – in short, it should be the attitude of an interested party. A double object is provided for the audience's interest. First, the events shown on stage; these must be of such a kind that they may, at certain decisive points, be checked by the audience against its own experience. Second, the production; this must be transparent as to its artistic armature. (Such transparency is the exact opposite of 'simplicity'; it presupposes genuine artistic intelligence and skill in the producer.) Epic theatre addresses itself to interested parties 'who do not think unless they have a reason to'. Brecht is contantly aware of the masses, whose conditioned use of the faculty of thought is surely covered by this formula. His effort to make the audience interested in the theatre as experts – not at all for cultural reasons – is an expression of his political purpose.

II The Fable (Story)

Epic theatre sets out 'to make what is shown on the stage unsensational'. Hence an old story will often be of more use to it than a new one. Brecht has considered the question whether the events shown in epic theatre ought not to be already known. The relationship of epic theatre to its story, he says, is like that of a ballet teacher to his pupil; his first task is to loosen her joints as far as they will go. (Chinese theatre proceeds in precisely this way. In 'The Fourth Wall of China'* Brecht has explained his debt to this theatre.) If theatre is to show events that are already known, 'then historical events would be, on the face of it, the most suitable'. The epic 'stretching' of these events by the method of acting, by posters and by captions aims at exorcizing their sensationalism.

Thus, in his latest play Brecht takes for his subject the life of Galileo. He represents Galileo first and foremost as a great teacher. Galileo not only teaches the new physics, he also teaches it in a new way. The scientific experiment is, in his hands, no longer a conquest only of science but also of pedagogy. The main emphasis of the play is not on Galileo's recantation. Rather, the really epic process should be sought in the caption to the penultimate scene: '1633–1642. As a prisoner of the Inquisition, Galileo continues his scientific work until his death. He succeeds in smuggling his principal works out of Italy.'

Epic theatre and tragic theatre have a very different kind of alli-

* *Life and Letters Today*, vol. XV, 1936, no. 6.

ance with the passing of time. Because the suspense concerns less
the ending than the separate events, epic theatre can span very ex-
tensive periods of time. (This was once equally true of the mystery
play. The dramaturgy of *Oedipus* or *The Wild Duck* is at the opposite pole to that of epic theatre.)

III The Untragic Hero

In French classical theatre there used to be a space left among the
actors for spectators of high rank, whose armchairs stood upon the
open stage. We think this out of place. The notion of 'the dramatic',
which is our accepted notion of the theatre, would make it appear
equally out of place if an impartial third party were associated, as
'the thinking man', with the events shown on stage. Yet something
like this has often occurred to Brecht. We may go further and say
that Brecht has attempted to make the thinking man, or indeed the
wise man, into an actual dramatic hero. And it is from this point of
view that his theatre may be defined as epic. The attempt is carried
furthest in the character of Galy Gay the packer. Galy Gay, the hero
of the play *A Man's a Man*, is himself like an empty stage on which
the contradictions of our society are acted out. Following Brecht's
line of thought, one might even arrive at the proposition that it is
the wise man who, in this sense, is the perfect empty stage. In any
case Galy Gay is a wise man. The undramatic nature of the highest
form of man – the sage – was clearly recognized by Plato a very long
time ago. In his dialogues he took the sage to the very threshold of
drama – in the *Phaedo*, to the threshold of the passion play. The
medieval Christ who, as we know from the Early Fathers, also
represented the sage, is the untragic hero *par excellence*. But in the
secular drama of the West, too, the search for the untragic hero has
never ceased. Often in conflict with its theoreticians, such drama has
deviated time and again, always in new ways, from the authentic
form of tragedy – that is, from Greek tragedy. This important but
badly marked road (which may serve here as the image of a tradition) ran, in the Middle Ages, via Hroswitha and the Mysteries; in
the age of the baroque, via Gryphius and Calderón. Later we find it

in Lenz and Grabbe, and finally in Strindberg. Shakespearian scenes stand as monuments at its edge, and Goethe crossed it in the second part of *Faust*. It is a European road, but it is a German one too. If, that is, one can speak of a road rather than a stalking-path along which the legacy of medieval and baroque drama has crept down to us. This stalking-path, rough and overgrown though it may be, is visible again today in the plays of Brecht.

IV The Interruptions

Brecht opposes his epic theatre to the theatre which is dramatic in the narrow sense and whose theory was formulated by Aristotle. This is why Brecht introduces the dramaturgy of his theatre as a 'non-Aristotelian' one, just as Riemann introduced a non-Euclidean geometry. This analogy should make it clear that what we have here is not a competitive relationship between the forms of drama in question. Riemann refused the axiom of parallels; what Brecht refuses is Aristotelian catharsis, the purging of the emotions through identification with the destiny which rules the hero's life.

The relaxed interest of the audience for which the productions of epic theatre are intended is due, precisely, to the fact that practically no appeal is made to the spectator's capacity for empathy. The art of epic theatre consists in arousing astonishment rather than empathy. To put it as formula, instead of identifying itself with the hero, the audience is called upon to learn to be astonished at the circumstances within which he has his being.

The task of epic theatre, Brecht believes, is not so much to develop actions as to represent conditions. But 'represent' does not here signify 'reproduce' in the sense used by the theoreticians of Naturalism. Rather, the first point at issue is to *uncover* those conditions. (One could just as well say: to *make them strange* [*verfremden*].) This uncovering (making strange, or alienating) of conditions is brought about by processes being interrupted. Take the crudest example: a family row. Suddenly a stranger comes into the room. The wife is just about to pick up a bronze statuette and throw it at the daughter, the father is opening the window to call a policeman.

At this moment the stranger appears at the door. 'Tableau', as they used to say around 1900. That is to say, the stranger is confronted with a certain set of conditions: troubled faces, open window, a devastated interior. There exists another point of view from which the more usual scenes of bourgeois life do not look so very different from this.

V The Quotable Gesture

'The effect of each sentence,' reads one of Brecht's dramaturgical didactic poems, 'was anticipated and revealed. And the moment was anticipated when the crowd would lay the sentences upon the scales.' In short, the action was interrupted. We may go further here and recall that interruption is one of the fundamental methods of all form-giving. It reaches far beyond the domain of art. It is, to mention just one of its aspects, the origin of the quotation. Quoting a text implies interrupting its context. It will readily be understood, therefore, that epic theatre, which depends on interruption, is quotable in a very specific sense. That its texts are quotable would be nothing very special. But the gestures used in the process of acting are another matter.

'Making gestures quotable' is one of the essential achievements of epic theatre. The actor must be able to space his gestures as the compositor produces spaced type. This effect can be achieved, for instance, by the actor on stage quoting a gesture of his own. Thus in *Happy End* we see that Carola Neher, in the role of a Salvation Army sergeant, after singing in a seamen's tavern in order to make converts there and choosing a song more appropriate to such a place than it would have been to a church, has to quote this song and the gestures with which she sang it in front of the Salvation Army Council. Or, in *The Measures Taken*, a group of Communists have to account before a Party tribunal for an action they have taken against another comrade. In doing so they not only repeat the event but also reproduce the gestures made by the other comrade. What in epic theatre as a whole is an artistic method of the subtlest kind is, in the *Lehrstück* (didactic play), put to immediate didactic use. At all events, epic theatre is, by definition, gestural. For the more often we interrupt someone in process of action, the more gestures we obtain.

VI The Didactic Play

Epic theatre is always intended for the actors quite as much as for the spectators. The essential reason why the didactic play falls into a category of its own is that, through the exceptional austerity of its apparatus, it facilitates and encourages the interchangeability of actors and audience, audience and actors. Every spectator can become one of the actors. And, of course, playing a 'teacher' is easier than playing a 'hero'.

In the first version of *The Flight of the Lindberghs*, which was published in a magazine, the aviator still appeared as hero. The play was devised for his glorification. The second version – and this is highly revelatory – owes its existence to a self-correction of Brecht's. What immense enthusiasm swept the two continents immediately after Lindbergh's flight! Yet the sensation soon fizzled out. In *The Flight of the Lindberghs* Brecht endeavours to break down the spectrum of the 'event' in order to extract the colours of 'experience': the experience which can only be drawn from Lindbergh's work (his flight), and which Brecht means to give back to 'the Lindberghs' (the workers).

T. E. Lawrence, the author of *The Seven Pillars of Wisdom*, wrote to Robert Graves upon joining the Royal Air Force that the step he had taken was for a man of today what entering a monastery had been for a man in the Middle Ages. In this statement we recognize the same type of tension which is characteristic of *The Flight of the Lindberghs* and of the later didactic plays. A monastic rigour is applied to the learning of a modern technique – in the one case that of flying, in the other that of the class struggle. This second application is carried through most thoroughly in *The Mother*. A social drama was a bold choice for refusing the effects of empathy to which modern audiences are so accustomed. Brecht is aware of this; he expresses it in an epistolary poem which he addressed to the workers' theatre in New York on the occasion of its production of the play, in the following terms: 'Many asked us: will the worker understand you? Will he agree to do without the usual drug of passive identification with other men's revolts, other men's victories? Will he give up the illusion which excites him for two hours and then leaves him more tired than ever, filled only with vague memories and vaguer hopes?'

VII   The Actor

Epic theatre proceeds by fits and starts, in a manner comparable to the images on a film strip. Its basic form is that of the forceful impact on one another of separate, sharply distinct situations in the play. The songs, the captions, the gestural conventions differentiate the scenes. As a result, intervals occur which tend to destroy illusion. These intervals paralyse the audience's readiness for empathy. Their purpose is to enable the spectator to adopt a critical attitude (towards the represented behaviour of the play's characters and towards the way in which this behaviour is represented). So far as the manner of representation is concerned, the task of the actor in epic theatre is to show, by his acting, that he is keeping a cool head. To him, too, empathy is of little use. For this way of acting, the 'actors' of dramatic theatre are not always and not completely prepared. By imagining what it means to 'play at acting' we may come closest to understanding what epic theatre is all about.

Brecht says: 'The actor must show an event, and he must show himself. He naturally shows the event by showing himself; and he shows himself by showing the event. Although these coincide, they must not coincide in such a way that the difference between the two tasks is lost.' In other words, the actor must reserve the right to act skilfully out of character. He must be free, at the right moment, to act himself thinking (about his part). It would be a mistake, at such moments, to draw a parallel with Romantic irony as practised, for example, by Tieck in *Puss in Boots*. This has no didactic purpose; in the final analysis, all it demonstrates is the philosophical sophistication of the author, who, while writing his plays, always has at the back of his mind the notion that the world may, after all, be just a stage.

It is precisely the manner of acting which, in epic theatre, can casually reveal the extent to which artistic interest is here identical with political interest. We need only think of Brecht's cycle *Terror and Misery of the Third Reich*. It is easy to see that the task of acting an SS man or a member of the People's Courts means something fundamentally different to a German actor in exile from what the task, say, of acting Molière's Don Juan would mean to a solid family man. For the former, empathy can scarcely be recommended as a suitable method, for there can be no empathy with the murderers of one's fellow-fighters. Such cases call for a new method whereby the actor distances himself from his role. The result could be extraordinarily successful; and the method would be the epic one.

VIII Theatre on the Public Platform

The concern of the epic theatre can be defined more readily in terms of the stage than in terms of a new kind of drama. Epic theatre takes account of a circumstance which has received too little attention, and which could be described as the filling-in of the orchestra pit. The abyss which separates the actors from the audience like the dead from the living, the abyss whose silence heightens the sublime in drama and whose resonance heightens the intoxication of opera – this abyss which, of all the elements of the stage, bears most indelibly the traces of its sacral origins, has increasingly lost its significance. The stage is still elevated. But it no longer rises from an immeasurable depth: it has become a public platform. The didactic play and epic theatre set out to occupy this platform.

STUDIES FOR A THEORY OF EPIC THEATRE

Epic theatre is gestural. Strictly speaking, the gesture is the material and epic theatre its practical utilization. If we accept this then two questions come to hand. First, from where does epic theatre obtain its gestures? Second, what do we understand by the 'utilization' of gestures? The third question which would then follow is: What methods does the epic theatre use in its treatment and critique of gestures?

In answer to the first question: the gestures are found in reality. More precisely – and this is an important fact very closely related to the nature of theatre – they are found only in the reality of today. Suppose that someone writes a historical play: we maintain that he will succeed in his task only to the extent that he is able to coordinate past events, in a meaningful and intelligible way, with gestures a man might make today. From this stipulation certain insights into the possibilities and limitations of historical drama might follow. In the first place, imitated gestures are worthless unless the point to be made is, precisely, the gestural process of imitation. Also, the gesture of, say, a pope as he crowns Charlemagne, or of Charlemagne as he receives the crown, can no longer occur today except as imitation. Hence the raw material of epic theatre is exclusively the gesture as it occurs today – the gesture either of an action or of the imitation of an action.

In answer to the second question: the gesture has two advantages over the highly deceptive statements and assertions normally made by people, and over their many-layered and opaque actions. First, the gesture is falsifiable only up to a point; and the more inconspicuous it is, the more habitually it is repeated, the more difficult it is to falsify. Secondly, unlike people's actions and endeavours, it has a definable beginning and a definable end. Indeed, this strict, frame-like, enclosed nature of each moment of an attitude which, after all, is as a whole in a state of living flux, is one of the basic dialectical characteristics of the gesture. This leads to an important conclusion: the more frequently we interrupt someone engaged in an action, the more gestures we obtain. Hence, the interrupting of action is one of the principal concerns of epic theatre. It is here that the importance of the songs for the 'economy' of the drama as a whole resides. Without anticipating the difficult study, yet to be made, of the function of the text in epic theatre, we can at least say that often its main function is not to illustrate or advance the action but, on the contrary, to interrupt it: not only the action of others, but also one's own. Incidentally, it is the retarding quality of these interruptions and the episodic quality of this framing of action which allow gestural theatre to become epic theatre.

A possible subject for further discussion might be the way in which the raw material (the gesture) thus prepared is processed on the stage. Action and text serve here as nothing more than variable elements in an experiment. But where does the result of the experiment point?

The answer to the second question, put in this way, cannot be separated from the problem of the third: what are the methods used in processing gestures?* These questions reveal the true dialectic of

* In the original typescript, the following passage appears in manuscript in the margin adjoining this paragraph: 'The gesture demonstrates the social significance and applicability of dialectics. It tests relations on men. The

epic theatre. We shall only point here to a few of its basic concepts. For a start, the following relationships are dialectical: that of the gesture to the situation, and *vice versa*; that of the actor to the character represented, and *vice versa*; that of the attitude of the actor, as determined by the authority of the text, to the critical attitude of the audience, and *vice versa*; that of the specific action represented to the action implied in any theatrical representation. This list is sufficient to show that all the dialectical moments are subordinated here to the supreme dialectic – now rediscovered after being forgotten for a long time – namely, the dialectic between recognition and education. All the recognitions achieved by epic theatre have a directly educative effect; at the same time, the educative effect of epic theatre is immediately translated into recognitions – though the specific recognitions of actors and audience may well be different from one another.

---

production difficulties which the producer meets while rehearsing the play cannot – even if they originate in the search for "effect" – be separated any longer from concrete insights into the life of society.'

FROM
THE
BRECHT
COMMENTARY

Bert Brecht is a difficult phenomenon. He refuses to make 'free' use of his great literary gifts. And there is not one of the gibes levelled against his style of literary activity – plagiarist, trouble-maker, saboteur – that he would not claim as a compliment to his unliterary, anonymous, and yet noticeable activity as educator, thinker, organizer, politician and theatrical producer. In any case he is unquestionably the only writer writing in Germany today who asks himself where he ought to apply his talent, who applies it only where he is convinced of the need to do so, and who abstains on every other occasion. The writings assembled under the title *Versuche* 1–3 are such points of application of his talent. The new thing here is that these points emerge in their full importance; that the author, for their sake, takes temporary leave of his *oeuvre* and, like an engineer starting to drill for oil in the desert, takes up his activity at precisely calculated places in the desert of contemporary life. Here these points are situated in the theatre, the anecdote, and radio; others will be tackled at a later stage. 'The publication of the *Versuche*,' the author begins, 'marks a point at which certain works are not so much meant to represent individual experiences (i.e. to have the character of finished works) as they are aimed at using (and transforming) certain existing institutes and institutions.' What is proposed here is not renovation, but innovation. Here literature no longer trusts any feeling of the author's which has not, in the desire to change the world, allied itself with sober intelligence. Here literature knows that the only chance left to it is to become a by-product in the highly ramified process of changing man's world. *Versuche* 1–3 is such a by-product, and an inestimable one; but the principal product is a new attitude. Lichtenberg said: 'It is not what a man is convinced of that matters, but what his convictions make of him.' This thing that a man's convictions make of him Brecht calls 'attitude'. 'The second *Versuch*, *Stories about Herr Keuner*,' says the author, 'represents an attempt to make gestures quotable.' Anyone who reads these stories will see that the gestures quoted are those of poverty, ignorance and impotence. The innovations introduced – patents, so to speak – are only small ones. Herr Keuner, a proletarian, is in sharp contrast to the ideal proletarian of the philanthropists: he is not interiorized. He expects the abolition of misery to arrive only by the logical development of the attitude which poverty forces upon him. Herr Keuner's attitude is not the only one that is quotable; the same applies to the disciples in *The Flight of the Lindberghs* and likewise to Fatzer the egoist. In each case what is quotable is not just the attitude but also the words which accompany it. These words, like gestures, must be practised, which is to say first noticed and later understood. They have their pedagogical effect first, their political effect second and their poetic effect last of all. The purpose of the commentary from which a sample is reproduced below is to advance the pedagogical effect as much as possible and to retard the poetic one.

I

Leave your post.
The victories have been gained.
    The defeats have been gained: 'The defeats have been gained . . .':

Now leave your post.

less by him, Fatzer, than for him. The victor must not allow the defeated the experience of defeat. He must snatch this, too; he must share defeat with the defeated. Then he will have become master of the situation.

Plunge back into the depths, conqueror.
Jubilation enters where the fighting was.
Be no longer there.
Wait for the cries of defeat where they are loudest:
In the depths.
Leave your old post.

'Plunge back . . .': 'No glory to the victor, no pity for the defeated.' Pokerwork inscription on a wooden plate, Soviet Russia.

Withdraw your voice, orator.
Your name is wiped off the tablets.
Your orders
Are not obeyed. Allow
New names to appear on the tablets and
New orders to be carried out.
(You who no longer command
Do not incite to disobedience!)
Leave your old post.

'Allow . . .': Here a harshness bordering on cruelty is permeated with courtesy. The courtesy is persuasive because one senses why it is there. It is there to induce the weakest and most worthless creature (to put it quite simply, man, in whom we recognize ourselves) to perform the greatest and most important action of all. It is the courtesy inherent in the act of sending a rope for a *harakiri*, an act whose wordlessness still leaves room for pity.

You were not up to it.
You did not bring it off
Now you have had experience and are up to it
Now you can start:

'Now you can start . . .': The 'start'

Leave your post.

is dialectically made new. It does not manifest itself in a fresh beginning but in a cessation. The action? The man must leave his post. Inward beginning == ceasing to do an outward thing.

You who ruled over ministries
Stoke your oven.
You who had no time to eat
Cook yourself some soup.
You about whom much is written
Study the ABC.
Make a start at once:
Take up your new post.

'You who ruled . . .': this is to emphasize the forces which the Soviet practice of moving officials round the various ministries releases in the person concerned. The command 'Start all over again' means, in dialectical terms: 1) learn, for you know nothing; 2) occupy yourself with fundamentals, for you have grown wise enough (through experience) to do so; 3) you are weak, you have been relieved of your post. Take it easy now so that you can get stronger; you have the time for it.

One who is beaten does not
      escape
Wisdom.
Hold on tight and sink! Be afraid!
      Go on, sink! At the bottom
The lesson awaits you.
You who were asked too many
      questions
Receive now the inestimable
Teaching of the masses:
Take up your new post.

'Go on, sink!': Fatzer must find a foothold in his hopelessness. A foothold, not hope. Consolation has nothing to do with hope. And Brecht offers him consolation: a man can live in hopelessness if he knows how he got there. He can live in it because his hopeless life is then of importance. To sink to the bottom here means always: to get to the bottom of things.

2

The table is finished, carpenter.
Allow us to take it away.
Stop planing it now
Leave off painting it
Speak neither well nor ill of it:
We'll take it as it is.
We need it.
Hand it over.

'Carpenter . . .': The carpenter we have to imagine here is an eccentric who is never satisfied with his 'work', who cannot make up his mind to let it out of his hands. If writers are taking temporary leave of their *oeuvre* (see above), then statesmen, too, are expected to show the same attitude. Brecht tells them: 'You are amateur craftsmen, you want to make the State your *oeuvre* instead of realizing that the State is not supposed to be a work of art, not an eternal value, but an object of practical use.'

You have finished, statesman.
The State is not finished.
Allow us to change it
To suit the conditions of life.
Allow us to be statesmen,
    statesman.
Beaneath your laws stands your
    name.
Forget the name
Respect your laws, legislator.
Submit to order, man of order.
The State no longer needs you
Hand it over.

'Hand it over': Here is what 'the Lindberghs' say of their machine: 'The thing they made will have to do for us.' Keep hard by hard reality: that is the order of the day. Poverty, so the bearers of knowledge teach, is a mimicry which brings the poor man closer to reality than any rich man can ever be.

A
FAMILY
DRAMA
IN THE
EPIC
THEATRE*

Brecht has said of Communism that it is 'the middle term'. 'Communism is not radical. It is capitalism that is radical.' How radical it is can be recognized, among other things, in its attitude towards the family. It insists upon the family at any price, even where any intensification of family life can only aggravate the suffering already caused by conditions utterly unworthy of human beings. Communism is not radical. Therefore it has no intention simply to abolish family relations. It merely tests them to determine their capacity for change. It asks itself: can the family be dismantled so that its components may be socially refunctioned? These components are not so much the members of the family themselves as their relationships with one another. Of these, it is clear that none is more important than the relationship between mother and child. Furthermore, the mother, among all family members, is the most unequivocally determined as to her social function: she produces the next generation. The question raised by Brecht's play is: can this social function become a revolutionary one, and how? In a capitalist

* On the occasion of the world première of Brecht's *The Mother*.

economic system, the more directly a person is engaged in production relations, the more he or she is subject to exploitation. Under the conditions of today, the family is an organization for the exploitation of the woman as mother. Pelagea Vlassova, 'widow of a worker and mother of a worker', is therefore someone who is doubly exploited: first, as a member of the working class, and second, as a woman and mother. The doubly exploited childbearer represents the exploited people in their most extreme oppression. If the mothers are revolutionized, there is nothing left to revolutionize.

Brecht's subject is a sociological experiment concerning the revolutionizing of a mother. This explains a number of simplifications which are not of an agitational but of a constructive kind. 'Widow of a worker, mother of a worker' – therein lies the first simplification. Pelagea Vlassova is the mother of only one worker, and for this reason she somewhat contradicts the original meaning of the word 'proletarian woman' (*proles* means descendants). This mother has only one son. The one is enough. For it turns out that with this one lever she can operate the mechanism which channels her maternal energies towards the entire working class. Her first duty is to cook. Producer of a man, she becomes the reproducer of his working strength. But there is no longer enough to eat for such reproduction. The son looks with contempt at the food she puts in front of him. How easily this look can wound the mother. She cannot help herself because she does not yet know that 'the decision about the meat lacking in the kitchen is not taken in the kitchen'. This, or something like it, is surely written in the leaflets she goes out to distribute. Not in order to help Communism, but to help her son who has to distribute them. This is how her work for the Party begins. And in this way she transforms the antagonism which threatened to develop between herself and her son into an antagonism against the enemy of them both. This unique attitude of the mother, this useful helpfulness which, as it were, resides in the folds of any mother's skirt, acquires now the social dimension (as solidarity of the oppressed) which it only possessed before in an animal sense. The road which the mother travels is that from the first kind of help to the ultimate, the solidarity of the working class.

Her speech to the mothers who queue up to hand in their copper kitchen-ware is not a pacifist one; it is a revolutionary exhortation to the childbearers who, by betraying the cause of the weak, also betray the cause of their own young, their children. And so we see that the mother's way to the Party starts first with help, and comes to theory only afterwards. This is the second constructive simplification. The purpose of these simplifications is to underline the simplicity of the lessons which they teach. It is in the nature of epic theatre to replace the undialectical opposition between the form and content of consciousness (which means that a character can only refer to his own actions by reflexions) by the dialectical one between theory and praxis (which means that any action that makes a breakthrough opens up a clearer view of theory). Epic theatre, therefore, is the theatre of the hero who is beaten. A hero who is not beaten never makes a thinker. Spare the rod and spoil the hero, to modify one of our forefathers' pedagogical maxims.

To consider now the 'lessons', the conclusions, with which the mother occupies herself during her times of defeat or of waiting (for epic theatre there is no difference between the two): they are like commentaries on her own attitude; and the special thing about them is that she sings them. She sings: What are the objections to Communism? She sings: Learn, woman of sixty. She sings: In Praise of the Third Cause. And she sings these songs as a mother. For they are lullabies. Lullabies for Communism, which is small and weak but irresistibly growing. This Communism she has taken unto herself as a mother. It becomes clear too that she is loved by Communism as only a mother is loved: she is loved not for the sake of her beauty or her fame or her excellence, but as the inexhaustible source of help; she represents help at its source, where it is still pure-flowing, where it is still practical and not false, from where it can still be channelled without reservation to that which, without reservation, needs help: namely, Communism. The mother is praxis incarnate. We see this when she makes tea, and we see it when she wraps up the pies; when she is visiting her son in prison we see that every single thing she does with her hands serves Communism; and when she is hit by stones and the policemen strike her with their rifle-butts, we see that whenever a hand is raised against her it is in vain.

The mother is praxis incarnate. This means that we shall not find enthusiasm in her but reliability. Yet she would not be reliable if she had not, at first, raised objections against Communism. But – and this is the decisive fact – her objections were not those of an interested party but those of common sense. 'It's necessary, therefore it isn't dangerous' – she'll never accept statements like that. And she has just as little use for utopias. 'Does Mr Sukhlinov own his factory or does he not? Well, then!' You can explain to her, however, that his ownership of the factory is a limited one. And so, step by step, she travels along the path of ordinary common sense. – 'If you've a disagreement with Mr Sukhlinov, what has that got to do with the police?' This step-by-step advance of ordinary common sense, the opposite of radicalism, leads the mother to the head of the May Day demonstration, where she is beaten down.

So much now for the mother. It is time to turn the tables and ask: if the mother leads, what is happening to the son? It is the son, after all, who reads books and prepares himself for leadership. There are four of them: mother and son, theory and praxis, and they regroup themselves, they play a game of change and change about. Once the critical moment arrives when ordinary common sense becomes the leader, theory is only just good enough to do the housework. The son must cut bread while the mother, who is illiterate, works the printing-press; the necessity of life no longer catalogues people according to their sex; in the worker's room a space is made between the kitchen range and the bed for a blackboard. When the State is turned upside down for the sake of a kopeck, much will change within the family, too, and at that moment the place of the bride, who personifies the ideals of the future, will be taken by the mother who, with all her forty years' experience, will confirm Marx and Lenin. The dialectic has no need of a far distance shrouded in mists: it is at home within the four walls of praxis, and it stands on the threshold of the moment to speak the closing words of the play: 'And "Never" becomes: "Before the day is out!"'

THE COUNTRY WHERE IT IS FORBIDDEN TO MENTION THE PROLETARIAT*

Only political drama can be the proper concern of theatre in emigration. Most of the plays which attracted a political audience ten or fifteen years ago have since been overtaken by events. The theatre of emigration must start again at the beginning; not just its stage, but also its plays must be built anew.

It was a sense of this historical situation which united the audience at the Paris première of parts of a new drama cycle by Brecht. The audience was recognizing itself for the first time as a dramatic audience. Taking account of this new audience and this new situation of the theatre, Brecht introduces a new dramatic form. He is an expert in fresh starts. In the years between 1920 and 1930 he never tired of testing his dramas against the example of contemporary history. In doing so he tried out numerous forms of theatre and the most varied types of public. He worked for the theatre of the public platform as well as for opera; he exhibited his products before the proletariat of Berlin as well as the bourgeois avant-garde of the West.

Thus, like no one else, Brecht started at the beginning again and

* On the world première of eight one-act plays by Brecht.

again. And this, incidentally, is the distinguishing mark of the dialectician. (There is a dialectician hidden in every master of an art.) Make certain, says Gide, that the impetus you have once achieved never benefits your subsequent work. Brecht has proceeded in accordance with this maxim – and particularly in the new plays intended for the theatre of emigration.

To sum up briefly: the 'attempts' (*Versuche*) of the earlier years yielded, in the end, a distinct and well-founded standard of Brechtian theatre. It described itself as epic, and, by this description, set itself up in opposition to the dramatic theatre whose theory was first formulated by Aristotle. That is why Brecht introduced his theory as 'non-Aristotelian', just as Riemann once introduced a 'non-Euclidean' geometry. Riemann rejected the axiom of parallels; what was rejected in this new drama was the Aristotelian 'catharsis', the purging of the emotions through identification with the hero's turbulent destiny: a destiny made turbulent by the movement of a wave which sweeps the audience along with it. (The famous *peripeteia* is the crest of the wave which, breaking, rolls forward to the end.)

Epic theatre, by contrast, advances by fits and starts, like the images on a film strip. Its basic form is that of the forceful impact on one another of separate, distinct situations in the play. The songs, the captions included in the stage decor, the gestural conventions of the actors, serve to separate each situation. Thus distances are created everywhere which are, on the whole, detrimental to illusion among the audience. These distances are meant to make the audience adopt a critical attitude, to make it think. (In a similar way the French classical stage made room among its actors for persons of high rank, whose arm-chairs were placed upon the open stage.)

Epic theatre overthrew certain crucial positions of bourgeois theatre by productions which were superior in method and precision to productions of the bourgeois theatre. But the victories it won were *ad hoc* ones. The epic stage was not yet so firmly established, and the circle of those trained to act upon it not yet so large, that it could be built up anew in emigration. Recognition of this fact lies at the root of Brecht's new work.

Terror and Misery of the Third Reich is a cycle formed of twenty-seven one-act plays constructed according to the precepts of traditional dramaturgy. Sometimes the dramatic element blazes out like á magnesium flare at the end of an apparently idyllic development. (Those who come in at the kitchen door are the Winter Aid* people with a sack of potatoes for the little household; those who walk out are storm troopers leading between them the daughter of the family, whom they have arrested.) Other parts of the cycle have fully developed dramatic plots (e.g. in *The Chalk Cross* a worker tricks a storm-trooper into revealing one of the methods which the Gestapo's accomplices use in fighting the underground). Sometimes it is the tension of a contradiction in social relations which, almost without transposition, is revealed dramatically on the stage. (Two prisoners taking exercise in the prison-yard under the eyes of the warder whisper among themselves; both are bakers; one is in gaol because he did not put any bran in his bread, the other was arrested a year later because he did.)

These and other plays were performed for the first time in S.Th. Dudow's well thought-out production on 21 May 1938 before an audience which followed them with passionate interest. At last, after five years of exile, the special political experience which unites this public found expression on a theatre stage. Steffi Spira, Hans Altmann, Günter Ruschin, Erich Schoenlank, actors who until then had not always been able to release their full potential when performing in individual numbers in political cabaret, now succeeded in playing off their talents against one another, and they showed to what good use they had put the experience which most of them had acquired nine months earlier in Brecht's *Señora Carrar's Rifles*.

Helene Weigel did justice to the tradition which, in spite of everything, has survived from Brecht's earlier work in this new kind of theatre. She maintained the kind of European authority established in the earlier Brechtian theatre. We would have given a great deal to see her in the last play of the cycle, *Referendum*, in which, as a proletarian woman (a part reminiscent of her unforgettable role in

* *Winterhilfe*: a spurious charity campaign mounted by the Nazi Party to ingratiate itself with the workers (Translator's note).

The Mother), she embodies the spirit of the underground struggle in times of persecution.

The cycle represents for the theatre of German emigration a political and artistic opportunity which palpably demonstrates, for the first time, the necessity for that theatre. The two elements, political and artistic, here merge into one. It is easy to see that to play a stormtrooper or a member of the 'people's courts' is a very different task for a refugee actor than it is, say, for a good-hearted actor to play Iago. For the former, empathy is no more suitable than it would be for a political fighter to identify himself with his comrades' murderer. A different mode of acting – the epic mode, to be plain – may find a new justification here and achieve a new kind of success.

The cycle – and here again its epic quality is apparent, though in a different form – can appeal to a reading public as much as to theatre audiences. As long as the conditions which Brecht depicts upon the stage prevail, it is unlikely that the means will be available for producing more than a fairly limited selection from the cycle. Such a selection is open to critical objections, and this goes for the Paris production. Not all the spectators were able to grasp what a reader would recognize as the determining thesis of all these short plays. The thesis can be summed up in a sentence from Kafka's prophetic *Trial*: 'The lie is transformed into a world order.'

Each of these short plays demonstrates one thing: how ineluctably the rule of terror which parades before the nations as the Third Reich makes all relationships between human beings subject to the law of the lie. A declaration under oath before a court of law is a lie (*Legal Finding*); a science whose teachings may not be applied in practice is a lie (*Occupational Disease*); what is shouted from the rooftops is a lie (*Referendum*) and what is whispered in a dying man's ears is still a lie (*The Sermon on the Mount*). A lie is brutally injected into what husband and wife have to say to one another in the last instants of their life together (*The Jewish Wife*); a lie is the mask which pity herself puts on when she still dares to give a sign of life (*In the Service of the People*). We are in the country where the name of the proletariat may not be mentioned. Brecht shows us how things have come to such a pass in that country that a peasant can-

not even any longer feed his beasts without endangering 'state
. security' (*The Farmer Feeds his Sow*).

The truth, which will one day consume this State and its order
like a purifying fire, is today only a feeble spark. It is fanned by the
worker who, in front of the microphone, shows up for the lies that
they are the words he is being forced to speak; it is kept alive by the
silence of those who cannot, except with the greatest circumspec-
tion, meet their comrade who has suffered martyrdom; whilst the
referendum leaflet whose entire text is 'NO' is nothing other than that
tiny glowing spark itself.

It is to be hoped that the cycle will soon be available in book form
For the stage it offers an entire repertoire. For the reader it is a drama
such as Kraus created in his *Last Days of Mankind*. It is only this
kind of drama which can perhaps contain the still glowing reality
of the present moment and carry it down to posterity like a testa-
ment of iron.

COMMENTARIES ON POEMS BY BRECHT

It is a known fact that a commentary is something different from a carefully weighed appreciation apportioning light and shade. The commentary proceeds from the classic nature of its text and hence, as it were, from a prejudgement. It is further distinguished from an appreciation by the fact that it is concerned solely with the beauty and the positive content of its text. And it is a very dialectical state of affairs which enlists this archaic form, the commentary – which, after all, is an authoritative form – in the service of a poetry which is not in the least archaic and which boldly challenges what is recognized as authoritative today.

Such a state of affairs coincides with one envisaged in an old maxim of dialectics: the surmounting of difficulties by their accumulation. The difficulty to be surmounted here consists in reading lyric poetry today at all. Supposing, then, that one tries to meet this difficulty by reading the text exactly as though it were an already established one, heavy with a content of ideas – in short, a classical text? And supposing – if one takes the bull by the horns, and if one bears in mind the special circumstance corresponding exactly to the difficulty of reading lyric poetry today, namely, the difficulty of writing lyric poetry today – supposing that, when we make our attempt to read a lyrical text as though it were a classical one, we choose a collection of *lyric verse written today?*

If anything can encourage this attempt, it is the recognition from which the courage of despair is generally drawn today: the recognition that tomorrow may bring disasters of such colossal dimensions that we can imagine ourselves separated from the texts and products of yesterday as though by centuries. (The commentary which today still fits the text too tightly may have loosened into classic folds tomorrow. Where today its precision may strike one as almost unseemly, tomorrow mystery may have re-established itself.)

Perhaps the commentary which follows will arouse interest in another way too. People for whom Communism appears to bear the stigma of onesidedness may have a surprise in store for them if they study closely a collection of verse such as Brecht's. The surprise will of course be lost if we insist on seeing only the 'development' which Brecht's verse has undergone from the *Hauspostille* to the *Svendborg Poems*. The asocial attitude of the *Hauspostille* is transformed, in the *Svendborg Poems*, into a social attitude. But that is not exactly a conversion. It is not a matter of consigning to the flames what once was worshipped. It is necessary to point out what the different collections of verse have in common. Among their multiple attitudes there is one you will never find: that is the unpolitical, non-social one. It is the commentary's purpose to pinpoint the political contents of passages chosen precisely because they are purely lyrical.

On the Hauspostille ('*Household Messenger*')

It goes without saying that the title 'Household Messenger' is ironic. Its message does not come down from Sinai or from the Gospels. The source of its inspiration is bourgeois society. The lessons which the careful reader draws from it differ as widely as possible from the lessons which it purports ostensibly to teach. The *Hauspostille* is concerned with the former category of lessons alone. If anarchy is the true law of bourgeois life, so reasons the poet, then let it at least be called by its proper name. None of the poetic forms with which the bourgeoisie embellishes its existence is too sacred for the poet to use in exposing the nature of bourgeois rule. The chorale which edifies the congregation, the folk-song which is fed as a sop to the people, the patriotic ballad that accompanies the soldier to the slaughter, the love-song that purveys the cheapest consolation – all of these receive here a new content, in that the irresponsible and asocial man speaks of these things (God, people, homeland and bride) in the way they should be spoken of in front of irresponsible and asocial men: without any false or true shame.

On the Mahagonny Songs*

MAHAGONNY SONG NO. 2

> Whoever stayed in Mahagonny
> Had to have five dollars a day
> And if he lived it up more than the others
> He needed some extra maybe
> But in those days they all stayed.
>
> They lost either way
>   But they got something out of it.

>   I

> On sea and on land
> Everybody's getting skinned
> That's why everybody you can see
> Is selling his skin
> For skins are worth dollars anyway.
>
>   Whoever stayed in Mahagonny
>   Had to have five dollars a day, etc.

* Unless otherwise indicated, the translations of verse in this volume are prose ones made by the translator. Others are reproduced from a projected volume of Brecht's verse in translation by courtesy of the editor, John Willett (Translator's note)

2

On sea and on land
Sales of fresh skins are booming
You've all got the itch
But who's going to pay for the booze?
For skins are cheap and whisky's dear.
 Whoever stayed in Mahagonny
 Had to have five dollars a day, etc.

3

On sea and on land
The many mills of God grind slow
And that's why everyone you can see
Is selling his skin
For they're fond of living high but they don't like paying cash.

 Whoever stays in his hole
 Doesn't need five dollars a day
 And if he's got a wife
 He doesn't need anything extra maybe.
 But today they're all sitting tight
 In God's own cheap saloon
 They win either way
 And they're getting nothing out of it.

MAHAGONNY SONG NO. 3

One grey morning
Right in the middle of the whisky
 God came to Mahagonny
 God came to Mahagonny.
 Right in the middle of the whisky
 We noticed God in Mahagonny.

I

Why do you soak up like sponges
My good wheat harvest year by year?

You never expected me to come
But now I'm here, is everything ready?
The men of Mahagonny looked at each other.
Yes, said the men of Mahagonny.

One grey morning
Right in the middle of the whisky, etc.

2

Do you laugh on Friday nights?
I saw Mary Weeman in the distance
Swimming like a codfish, dumb, in the salt sea.
Gentlemen, she'll be dry no more.
The men of Mahagonny looked at each other.
Yes, said the men of Mahagonny.

One grey morning
Right in the middle of the whisky, etc.

3

Do you recognize these bullets?
Was it you who fired at my good missionary?
Am I going to live with you in heaven?
Am I going to gaze upon your grey drunkards' hair?
The men of Mahagonny looked at each other.
Yes, said the men of Mahagonny.

One grey morning
Right in the middle of the whisky, etc.

4

All of you are going to hell!
Put your Virginia cigars away!
Off to hell, the lot of you,
Black hell's your lot!
The men of Mahagonny looked at each other.
Yes, said the men of Mahagonny.
One grey morning
Right in the middle of the whisky

You turn up in Mahagonny
You turn up in Mahagonny.
Right in the middle of the whisky
You lay down the law in Mahagonny!

5

Nobody move!
Everyone on strike!
You won't drag us to hell by our hair:
For we've been in hell all along.
The men of Mahagonny looked at God.
No, said the men of Mahagonny.

The 'men of Mahagonny' are a band of eccentrics. Only men are
eccentrics. Only persons endowed by nature with male potency can
be used to demonstrate without limitation the degree to which the
natural reflexes of human beings have been blunted by their existence
in the society of today. The eccentric is nothing other than the average man, played out. Brecht has combined several into a band. Their
reactions are the most blurred possible, and even these they can only
produce as a collective. In order to be able to react at all they have to
feel themselves a 'compact mass' – and in this too they are the image
of the average man, alias petty bourgeois. The 'men of Mahagonny'
look at one another before they say anything. The response which
they then bring out lies along the line of least resistance. The 'men
of Mahagonny' confine themselves to saying 'yes' to everything
God tells them, to every question God puts to them and every
demand he makes upon them. Such, according to Brecht, must be
the nature of a collective that accepts God. And this God too is
himself a reduced one. The words

We noticed God

in the refrain of Song No. 3 imply it, and its last verse confirms it.
The first assent is given to the statement:

You never expected me to come.

It is clear, however, that the blunted reactions of the men of Mahagonny are not sharpened even by the surprise effect. In a similar way, later on, they seem to think that their claim to enter heaven is in no way weakened by the fact that they have fired at the missionary. The fourth verse reveals that God's view is different:

> *Off to hell, the lot of you!*

Here is the hinge, dramaturgically speaking the *peripeteia*, of the poem. In issuing his command God has made a blunder. To measure its extent it is necessary to visualize the locality a little more clearly. It is defined in the final verse of Song No. 2. In fact, with the image of this definition of a place, the poet addresses his epoch.

> *But today they're all sitting tight*
> *In God's own cheap saloon.*

The adjective 'cheap' contains a good deal of meaning (*Translator's note*: the German word *billig* means 'fair' or 'just' as well as 'cheap'; the verb *billigen* means 'to sanction' or 'to approve'). Why is the saloon cheap? It is cheap because the people in it are God's guests at a cheap price. It is cheap (*billig*) because the people approve (*billigen*) everything that is in it. It is cheap (fair) because it is fair that people should enter it. God's own cheap saloon is hell. The expression has the terse quality of certain drawings by the insane. It is just like this, as a cheap saloon, that the man in the street (once he has gone mad) may well picture the little plot of heaven which is accessible to him. (Abraham à Santa Clara might have spoken of 'God's cheap saloon'.) But God in his own cheap saloon has made himself cheap with the habitués. His threat of sending them to hell has no more value than a publican's threat to throw his customers out into the street.

The 'men of Mahagonny' have realized this. Not even they are so brainless as to be impressed by the threat of being sent to hell. The anarchy of bourgeois society is an infernal one. For human beings who have been caught up in it, something that fills them with greater horror than this society simply cannot exist.

You won't drag us to hell by our hair:
For we've been in hell all along.

says the third Mahagonny song. The only difference between hell and this social order is that in the petty bourgeois (the eccentric) there is no rigid distinction between his own poor soul and the Devil.

On the poem 'Against Deception'

AGAINST DECEPTION

Let them not deceive you
There is no returning home.
The day is nearly over
The night wind makes you shiver
Tomorrow will not come.

Let them not mislead you
With vanity and woe.
Gulp life with urgent greed; you
'll find nothing else to feed you
When once you let it go.

Let them not hear you crying
You have so little time.
Decay is for the dying
Life's climax now is flying
It will not stay the same.

Let them not defeat you
Or shape you as they want.
No terrors now can reach you
You'll die like any creature
And nothing waits beyond.

translated by John Willett

The poet grew up in a suburb with a predominantly Catholic population; but the petty-bourgeois element there was already becoming mixed with workers from the large factories on the outskirts of the town. This explains the attitude and vocabulary of the poem 'Against Deception'. The people have been warned by the clergy against temptations for which they will have to pay dearly in a second life after death. The poet warns them against temptations and deceptions for which they must pay dearly in this life here on earth. He contests the existence of another life. His warning is given no less solemnly than that of the clergy; his assurances are equally apodictic. Like the clergy, he employs the concept of 'deception' (or 'temptation') absolutely, without adjunct; he takes over their edifying accents. The elevated tone of the poem may seduce the reader into glossing over certain passages which lend themselves to different interpretations and contain a kind of hidden beauty.

There is no returning home.

First interpretation: let them not deceive you into believing that there is a return home. Second interpretation: take care not to make any mistakes, for you only live once.

The day is nearly over (Translator's note: the literal rendering of the German line, *Der Tag steht in den Türen*, is: 'The day stands in the door').

First interpretation: the day is ready to go, it is departing. Second interpretation: the day is at its height (yet, even so, you can already feel the breath of the night wind).

Tomorrow will not come.

First interpretation: there will not be another day. Second interpretation: there will not be another morning (*Translator's note:* the German *Morgen* means both 'tomorrow' and 'morning', cf. the English 'morrow'). The night has the last word.

Das Leben wenig ist (Translator's note: this line, the second of the second verse, is lost in the above translation, to allow the rhyme 'woe - go'. The literal meaning is: 'Life is a small thing.').

In the Kiepenheuer private edition this line read *Daß Leben wenig ist* ('that life is a small thing'). This version differs from the later, public one in two respects. The first difference is that the earlier version extends and defines the first line of this verse ('Let them not deceive you') by spelling out the thesis of the deceivers, i.e. that life is a small thing. The second difference is to be seen in the fact that the line 'Life is a small thing' expresses the wretchedness of life in an incomparable way and thus underlines the exhortation not to be argued out of any of it.

It will not stay the same (Translator's note: the literal meaning of the German, *Es steht nicht mehr bereit*, is: 'It stands ready no more.').

First interpretation: 'It stands ready *no more*': this adds nothing to the preceding line, 'Life's climax is now flying'. Second interpretation: 'It stands *ready* no more': you have already half-missed this, your greatest chance. Your life stands ready for you no more; it has already begun, has already been staked in the game.

The poem forces us to be shaken, or shattered, by the shortness of our life. One would do well to ponder the fact that the German word *erschüttern* ('to shake') conceals in it the word *schütter* ('sparse'). Where something collapses, there are bound to be holes and gaps. Analysis shows that in this poem there are numerous passages where the words combine but loosely and **unstead**ily to yield a meaning. This intensifies the poem's shattering **effect**.

On the poem 'Of the Sinners in Hell'

OF THE SINNERS IN HELL

I

> The sinners in hell
> Fry hotter than you think
> But if you weep for one
> The tear falls gently on his head.

2

They who burn the blackest
Get no tears from any one
On their day off they go out
To beg for a tear.

3

They stand there invisible.
The wind goes through their bodies
The sun shines through them.
They cannot be seen.

4

Here comes our Müllereisert
He died in America
His bride doesn't know it yet
That's why water there is none.

5

And here is Kaspar Neher
He comes as soon as the sun breaks through
And nobody, God knows why,
Ever sheds a tear for him.

6

Then comes George Pfanzelt
A most unhappy man
His idea was that
He did not matter.

7

And sweet Marie there
She rotted away in hospital
And never gets a tear.
She cared too little about it all.

8

And there in the light stands Bert Brecht
Over there by a dog-stone.
He gets no water because everyone thinks
He's gone to heaven.

9

Yet he's burning now in hell
Weep my brothers weep
Or every Sunday afternoon
He must stand there by his dog-stone.

This poem shows with startling clarity the great distance from which the poet of the *Household Messenger* has travelled. Now, having come so far, he reaches casually for the nearest thing at hand. The nearest thing at hand is Bavarian folk-lore. The poem lists friends in hell-fire in the same way as a shrine at the roadside may commend those who died without receiving the last sacraments to the prayers of passers-by. Yet the poem which at first glance appears so narrowly confined comes, in reality, from very far away. Its pedigree is that of the lament, which was one of the major forms of medieval literature. One could say that it goes back to the ancient lament in order to lament something very modern: the fact that even lamentation has become a thing of the past.

> *Here comes our Müllereisert*
> *He died in America*
> *His bride doesn't know it yet*
> *That's why water there is none.*

True, the poem does not properly lament this tearlessness. Nor can one properly assume that Müllereisert is dead, since, according to the author's 'instructions', this section of the book is dedicated to him – not to his memory.

The shrine which is put here bears images of the friends in hell-fire who are mentioned by name; but at the same time (this can be done in a poem) it addresses them as passers-by in order to remind them that they can expect no intercession. The poet carries this out with perfect composure. But at the end his composure fails him. He comes to speak of his own poor soul, forlorn like no other. It stands in the light and, what is more, on a Sunday afternoon and by a dog-stone. Just what that is one does not quite know; perhaps a stone against which dogs make water. For this sinner's soul, that would be something as familiar as a damp patch on the wall of his cell is for a prisoner. With the poet himself the joke comes to an end, and having shown so much insolence he begs – insolently, it is true – for tears.

On the poem 'Of Poor B.B.'

OF POOR B.B.

I, Bertolt Brecht, come out of the black forests.
My mother brought me to the cities early on
As I lay in her body. And the chill of the forest
Will remain with me till my life is done.

In the asphalt city I am at home. From the first
Supplied with Extreme Unction in plenty:
With papers. Tobacco. And brandy.
Mistrustful and idle, and ultimately not discontented.

I am polite to people. I wear
A hard hat in order to look like the others.
I say: what curious-smelling animals,
Then I think: I'm one myself; so why bother?

In my empty rocking-chairs before luncheon
I place one or two women I've my eye on,
And I look them over carelessly and tell them:
Here you've a man you can't rely on.

Towards evening I get some men together,
We start addressing each other as 'gentlemen'.
They put their feet up on my tables
Saying: It'll work out all right. I don't ask: When?

Towards morning in the grey light the pinetrees stand pissing.
And the vermin in them – birds – begin to screech.
About that hour I'm emptying my glass in the city and throwing
My cigarette-butt away; and drop restlessly to sleep.

A makeshift race, we came and settled
In houses that were supposed to last
(Thus we built the tall containers on Manhattan Island
And the slender antennae on which the Atlantic rests).

Will survive of these cities what went through them: the wind!
The banqueter is glad to empty the mansion.
We realize that we are purely provisional
And after us will come – nothing worth mention.

In the earthquakes that are to follow I greatly hope
I shan't grow too embittered to puff at my cigar
I, Bertolt Brecht, adrift in the asphalt cities
Long ago, in my mother, from where the black forests are.

translated by John Willett

I, Bertolt Brecht, come out of the black forests.
My mother brought me to the cities early on
As I lay in her body. And the chill of the forest
Will remain with me till my life is done.

In the forests it is cold, it cannot be any colder in the cities. Already in his mother's body the poet was as cold as in the asphalt cities in which he was to live.

About that hour I'm emptying my glass in the city and
Throwing my cigarette-butt away; and drop restlessly to sleep.

Perhaps not the last thing which provokes this restlessness is the thought of sleep itself, body-relaxing, rest-giving sleep. Will it deal more kindly with the sleeper than the mother's womb dealt with the unborn? Probably not. Nothing makes sleep so unquiet as the fear of waking.

(Thus we built the tall containers on Manhattan Island
And the slender antennae on which the Atlantic rests).

The antennae (aerials) which 'support' (or entertain) the Atlantic do not, we may be sure, entertain it with music or talk but with short and long waves, with the molecular processes which are the physical existence of radio. In this line the utilization of technical media by modern man is dismissed with a shrug of the shoulders.

Will survive of these cities what went through them: the wind!

If the wind that went through them survives these cities, it will no longer be the old wind that knew nothing of cities. The cities with their asphalt, with their streets and many windows will, when destroyed and disintegrated, dwell in the wind.

The banqueter is glad to empty the mansion.

The banqueter here represents the destroyer. Eating is not only feeding oneself, it is also digging one's teeth into something and destroying it. The world is immensely simplified if we test it, not so much for its enjoyability (edibility), as for its destructibility. Destructibility is the bond that unites in harmony everything that exists. The sight of this harmony fills the poet with joy. He is the banqueter with the iron jaws who empties the world's mansion.

> *We realize that we are purely provisional*
> *And after us will come – nothing worth mention.*

Vorläufige, 'provisional' – perhaps they might be *Vorläufer*, 'precursors'; but how can they be, since nothing worth mentioning will come after them? It is not entirely their fault if they go down in history without glory. (The poem 'To our Successors', written ten years later, takes up a similar thought.)

> *I, Bertolt Brecht, adrift in the asphalt cities*
> *Long ago, in my mother, from where the black forests are.*

The piling-up of prepositions of place – three in two lines – must produce an uncommonly disturbing effect. The straggling time clause 'long ago' (*Translator's note*: in the German this clause comes at the end of the last line) has doubtless missed its connection with the present and so reinforces an impression of powerlessness, of abandonment. The poet speaks as if, already in his mother's womb, he had been exposed to every wind.

Whoever reads this poem has walked through the poet as through a gate upon which, in weather-worn letters, a B.B. can be deciphered. The poet wants to halt the reader on his way as little as a gate wants to halt the passer-by. The archway was, perhaps, built centuries ago: it still stands because it stood in no one's way. If he stands in no one's way, B.B. will do justice to his nickname (*poor* B.B.). Nothing worth mentioning can happen in the life of someone who stands in no one's way and who no longer matters – unless it be the decision to put oneself in people's way and to make sure that one does matter. The later cycles of poems bear witness to just such a decision. Their cause is the class struggle. The best defender of a cause is one who has made a start by letting go of himself.

On the Studies

These *Studies* are not so much the products of industrious zeal as of an *otium cum dignitate*. Sometimes an engraver's hand, scarcely moving, will draw or doodle images at the edge of the plate; in the same way images from earlier times are here recorded in the margin of Brecht's work. It happens to the poet that, looking up from his work, he may glance across the present into the past. 'For the compact garlands of the sonnet/Weave themselves as though of their own accord in my hands/Whilst my eyes graze in the distance,' says Mörike. A casual glance into the distance, whose findings are enclosed in the strictest poetic form.

Among the later poetic works, the *Studies* are especially akin to the *Household Messenger*. The *Household Messenger* objects to much of our morality; it has reservations regarding a number of traditional commandments. It has not the remotest intention, however, of explicitly stating these reservations. It brings them out in the form of variants, precisely, of the moral attitude and gestures whose customary form it considers to be no longer quite fitting. In the *Studies* Brecht treats a number of literary documents and works in a similar spirit. He has reservations about them. But by translating these reservations into sonnet form he puts them to the test. That they survive this treatment proves their validity.

In the *Studies* reserve is mixed with a certain amount of reverence. The unreserved tribute, which corresponds to a barbarian contempt of culture, has made room for a tribute full of reservations.

On the Handbook for City-dwellers

THE FIRST POEM FROM THE *Handbook for City-dwellers*

Part from your friends at the station
Enter the city in the morning with your coat buttoned up
Look for a room, and when your friend knocks:
Do not, oh do not, open the door
But
Cover your tracks.

If you meet your parents in Hamburg or elsewhere
Pass them like strangers, turn the corner, don't recognize them
Pull the hat they gave you over your face, and
Do not, oh do not, show your face
But
Cover your tracks.

Eat the meat that's there. Don't stint yourself.
Go into any house when it rains and sit on any chair that's in it
But don't sit long. And don't forget your hat.
I tell you:
Cover your tracks.

Whatever you say, don't say it twice
If you find your ideas in anyone else, disown them.
The man who hasn't signed anything, who has left no picture
Who was not there, who said nothing:
How can they catch him?
Cover your tracks.

See when you come to think of dying
That no gravestone stands and betrays where you lie
With a clear inscription to denounce you

And the year of your death to give you away.
Once again:
Cover your tracks.

(That is what they taught me).

translated by Frank Jellinek

Arnold Zweig has pointed out that this sequence of poems has acquired a new meaning in recent years; it represents the city as the refugee experiences it in a foreign country. That is correct. But one should not forget that the man who fights for the exploited class is a refugee in his own country. For the intelligent Communist, the final five years of his political work in the Weimar Republic signified a crypto-emigration. Brecht experienced those years as such. This may have provided the immediate occasion for the writing of this cycle of poems. Crypto-emigration was a preliminary form of actual emigration; it was also a preliminary form of underground political activity.

Cover your tracks

A precept for the underground political worker!

If you find your ideas in anyone else, disown them.

A curious precept for the intellectual of 1928, a crystal-clear one for the intellectual gone underground.

See when you come to think of dying
That no gravestone stands and betrays where you lie

– this precept alone could be considered out of date; the underground political workers have been relieved of this worry by Hitler and his thugs.

In this handbook the city is seen as the arena of the struggle for existence and of the class struggle. The vision of the one is rather anarchistic and has links with the *Household Messenger*; the vision of the second is revolutionary and points forward to the 'Three Soldiers', its successor. In each case one thing remains unchanged:

cities are battlefields. One cannot imagine an observer less sensitive to the beauties of landscape than the strategically trained observer of a battle. One cannot imagine an observer surveying the charms of a city – its multitude of houses, the breath-taking speed of its traffic, its entertainments – more unfeelingly than Brecht. This lack of feeling for the city décor, combined with an extreme sensibility for the city-dweller's special ways of reaction, distinguishes Brecht's cycle from all big-city poetry that precedes it. Walt Whitman intoxicated himself with the human masses; of these there is no mention in Brecht. Baudelaire perceived the frailty at the heart of Paris; in the Parisians he perceived only what that frailty had done to them. Verhaeren attempted an apotheosis of cities. To Georg Heym they appeared full of portents of the catastrophes which threatened them.

Important big-city poetry generally left out the city-dweller. He may be there in Dehmel, but in this case the admixture of petty-bourgeois illusions proved fatal to poetic success. Brecht is probably the first important poet who has something to say about urban man.

On the third poem from the Handbook for City-Dwellers

We do not want to leave your house
We do not want to smash the stove
We want to put the pot on the stove.
House, stove and pot can stay
And you must vanish like smoke in the sky
Which nobody holds back.

If you want to cling to us we'll go away
If your woman weeps we'll put our hats over our faces
But when they come for you we shall point
And shall say: That must be him.

We don't know what's to come, and have nothing better
But we want no more of you.
Until you've gone
Let us draw the curtains to shut out tomorrow.

The cities are allowed to change
But you are not allowed to change.

We shall argue with the stones
But you we shall kill
You must not live
Whatever lies we are forced to believe
You must not have been.

(That is how we speak to our fathers.)

translated by Frank Jellinek

The expulsion of Jews from Germany was (until the pogroms of 1938) carried out in the spirit described in this poem. The Jews were not murdered immediately, wherever they happened to be found. Rather, they were dealt with in accordance with this principle:

We do not want to smash the stove
We want to put the pan on the stove.
House, stove and pot can stay
And you must vanish . . .

Brecht's poem is illuminating for the reader of today. It shows very clearly why National Socialism needs anti-semitism. It needs it as a parody. The attitude which the rulers artificially provoke *vis-à-vis* the Jews is precisely the one which would be natural in the oppressed class *vis-à-vis* the rulers. The Jew – Hitler ordains – shall be treated as the great exploiter ought to have been treated. And just because this treatment of the Jew is not really in earnest, because it is the distorted mirror-image of a genuine revolutionary action, it includes an admixture of sadism. The parody cannot do without sadism. The purpose of this parody is to make a mockery of the historical proposition that the expropriators shall be expropriated.

On the ninth poem from the Handbook for City-Dwellers

FOUR INVITATIONS TO A MAN AT DIFFERENT TIMES
FROM DIFFERENT QUARTERS

There's a home for you here
There's room for your things.

Move the furniture about to suit yourself
Tell us what you need
Here is the key
Stay here.

There's a parlour for us all
And for you a room with a bed
You can work with us in the yard
You have your own plate
Stay with us.

Here's where you're to sleep
The sheets are still clean
They've only been slept in once.
If you're fussy
Rinse your tin spoon in the bucket there
It'll be as good as new
You're welcome to stay with us.

That's the room
Hurry up, or you can also stay
The night, but that costs extra.
I shan't disturb you
By the way, I'm not ill.
You'll be as well off here as anywhere else
So you might as well stay.

translated by Frank Jellinek

The *Handbook for City-Dwellers* provides, as we have already said, object lessons in underground activity and emigration. The ninth poem is concerned with a social process which underground political workers as well as emigrants have to share with those who succumb to exploitation without struggle. The poem illustrates with a few economical strokes what impoverishment in a large city means. At the same time it sheds light upon the first poem of the cycle.

Each of the 'Four Invitations to a Man at Different Times from Different Quarters' enables us to recognize the man's particular economic situation. He gets steadily poorer. The people who offer to put him up take this as said; they allow him progressively less right to leave any tracks. The first time they still take notice of his belongings. On the second occasion only a plate of his own is mentioned, and this is hardly likely to be a plate he has brought with him. The lodger's labour power is already being disposed of by the landlord ('You can work with us in the yard'). The man who appears in the third verse is probably entirely unemployed. The private sphere of his life is symbolically represented by the act of washing a tin spoon. The fourth invitation is from a prostitute to a customer who is obviously poor. Nor is there any longer any question of duration. It is a lodging for one night at most, and the tracks which the man addressed may leave behind are best unmentioned. For the reader of the ninth poem, the precept of the first – 'Cover your tracks' – is supplemented by the adjunct: 'rather than have someone else cover them'.

The friendly indifference which is common to all four invitations is worthy of note. By the fact that the harshness of the offer leaves room for such friendliness we recognize that social conditions confront man from outside, as something alien to him. The friendliness with which their verdict is communicated to him by his fellow men shows that they do not feel identified with those conditions. The man addressed appears to accept what he is told: likewise, those who address him have come to terms with the conditions of life. The inhumanity to which they are condemned has not been able to take from them a certain courtesy of the heart. This may serve as justification for hope or despair. The poet does not express any views on this score.

On the Svendborg Poems *and on the* German War Primer

5

The workers cry out for bread
The merchants cry out for markets.
The unemployed were hungry. The employed
Are hungry now.
The hands that lay folded are busy again:
They are making shells.

translated by H. R. Hays

13

It is night. The married couples
Lie in their beds. The young women
Will bear orphans.

translated by Lee Baxandall

15

Those at the top say:
It leads to glory.
Those down below say:
It leads to the grave.

translated by Carol Stewart and John Willett

18

When it comes to marching many do not know
That their enemy is marching at their head.
The voice which gives them their orders
Is the enemy's voice and
The man who speaks of the enemy
Is the enemy himself.

translated by Carol Stewart and John Willett

The *War Primer* is written in 'lapidary' style. The word comes
from the Latin *lapis*, 'stone', and describes the style which was developed for Roman inscriptions. Its most important characteristic
was brevity. This was conditioned, first, by the effort required to
chisel the words in stone; second, by the realization that for one who
speaks to a succession of generations it is seemly to be brief.

If stone – the natural condition of lapidary style – is no longer the
material of these poems, what has taken its place? What justifies
their inscription style? One of them hints at an answer. It reads:

On the wall was chalked:
They want war.
The man who wrote it
Has already fallen.

translated by Carol Stewart and John Willett

The first line of this poem could be placed at the head of each of the *War Primer* poems. These inscriptions are not, like those of the Romans, intended for stone but, like those of underground fighters, for fences.

Accordingly, the character of the *War Primer* may be seen in a unique contradiction: these words, whose poetic form implies that they are meant to survive the forthcoming end of the world, contain the gesture of a slogan scrawled in haste on a plank fence by a man being pursued. In this contradiction lies the extraordinary artistic achievement of these sentences constructed out of primitive words. The poet endows with the Horatian *aere perennis* what a proletarian, exposed to the rain and the agents of the Gestapo, has scrawled with chalk upon a wall.

On the poem 'The Child Who Didn't Want to Wash'

THE CHILD WHO DIDN'T WANT TO WASH

Once there was a child
Who didn't want to wash.
And when they'd got him washed
He'd rub his face in ash.

The Kaiser came to call
Up seven flights of stairs.
Mother looked for a towel
To clean his face and hair.

There was no rag about.
The whole visit was wrecked.
The Kaiser went away.
What could the child expect?

translated by Anna Bostock and Peter Levi

The poet sides with the child who didn't want to wash. He suggests that the craziest circumstances would have to conspire for the child to suffer any real harm as a result of its unwashed condition.

Not only is it most unusual for the Kaiser to take the trouble to climb seven flights of stairs: but, as if that weren't enough, he has to choose to visit a household in which even a rag cannot be found. The fragmented diction of the poem implies that such a concatenation of accidents has something dreamlike about it.

Perhaps we might call to mind another partisan or defender of unwashed children: Fourier, whose phalanstery was not only a socialist utopia but also a pedagogical one. Fourier divides the children of the phalanstery into two major groups: the *petites bandes* and the *petites hordes*. The *petites bandes* occupy themselves with gardening and other pleasant tasks. The *petites hordes* have to perform the dirtiest duties. The choice between the two groups is open to every child. Those who opted for the *petites hordes* were the most honoured. No work could be undertaken in the phalanstery without their first having their say about it; cruelty to animals was subject to their jurisdiction; they had dwarf ponies on which they galloped through the phalanstery, and when they assembled for work the signal was given by an ear-shattering din of trumpets, steam-whistles, church bells and drums. In the children of the *petites hordes* Fourier saw four great passions at work: arrogance, shamelessness and insubordination; but the most important of all was the fourth: *le goût de la saleté*, a taste for dirt.

The reader thinks again of the child who would not wash and wonders: perhaps it only rubs its face in ash because society has failed to channel its passion for dirt towards a good and useful purpose? Perhaps it only wants to stand in society's way like a stumbling-block, so as to issue a mysterious warning – like the little hunchback in the German nursery song, who upsets every orderly household? If Fourier is right, then the child would surely not have missed a great deal by failing to meet the Kaiser. A Kaiser who only wants to see clean children doesn't amount to much more than the stupid subjects on whom he comes to call.

On the poem 'The Plum Tree'

THE PLUM TREE

> The plum tree in the yard's so small
> It hardly seems a tree at all.
> Yet there it is, railed round
> To keep it safe and sound.
>
> The poor thing can't grow any more
> Though if it could it would for sure.
> There's nothing to be done
> It gets too little sun.
>
> The plum tree never bears a plum
> So it's not easy to believe.
> It's a plum tree all the same
> You tell it by the leaf.

translated by Carol Stewart

The way in which landscape comes into the various cycles in Brecht's book exemplifies the inner unity of this lyric poetry and, at the same time, its wealth of perspectives. In the *Household Messenger*, landscape occurs above all in the form of a sky that has been purified, as though washed clean, upon which delicate clouds appear from time to time and beneath which vegetation outlined with a hard pencil may be visible. In *Songs Poems Choruses* nothing is left of landscape; it is covered by the 'wintry snowstorm' that sweeps through this cycle of poems. In the *Svendborg Poems* it is glimpsed now and again, timid and pale: so pale that the posts 'put up in the yard for the children's swing' already count as part of it.

The landscape of the *Svendborg Poems* resembles the one preferred by Herr Keuner in a story by Brecht. Friends have heard him say that he is fond of the tree that is wasting away in the yard of the tenement house in which he lives. They invite him to come with them to the woods, and are surprised because Herr Keuner declines to do so. Did you not say that you like trees? Herr Keuner replies: 'I said I liked the tree *in my yard*.' This tree may well be identical with the one which, in the *Household Messenger*, goes by the name of *Green*.* The poet honours it by addressing it in the morning, as follows:

> It can't have been a trifling thing to grow so high
> Between the houses
> To grow so high, Green, that the
> Storm visited you as it did last night?

This tree, Green, which offers its tree-top to the storm, still belongs to a 'heroic landscape'. (The poet, however, distances himself from this landscape by addressing the tree formally as *Sie*.) As the years pass, Brecht's lyrical eye turns to that aspect of the tree which resembles the human beings whose windows face the yard in which it stands: the mediocre and the stunted. A tree that no longer has anything heroic about it appears in the *Svendborg Poems* as a plum tree. A railing has to protect it from being kicked crooked. It bears no plums.

> *The plum tree never bears a plum*
> *So it's not easy to believe.*
> *It is a plum tree all the same*
> *You tell it by the leaf.*

(The internal rhyme in the first line [*den Pflaumenbaum glaubt man ihm kaum*] renders the last word of the third line [*Pflaumenbaum*] unsuitable for further rhyming; it indicates that for the plum tree, although it has scarcely begun to grow, life is already over.)

That is what the tree in the yard which Herr Keuner was fond of looks like. The only traces it still bears of landscape and everything that it once offered to a lyric poet is a single leaf. Perhaps, too, one has to be a great lyric poet today in order not to reach out for more.

* In English in the original (Translator's note).

On *the* 'Legend of the Origin of the Book Tao Te Ching on Lao
  Tzu's Way into Exile'

LEGEND OF THE ORIGIN OF THE BOOK TAO TE CHING
ON LAO TZU'S WAY INTO EXILE

1

When he was seventy and growing frail
The teacher after all felt the need for peace
For once again in the country kindness did not prevail
And malice once again was on the increase.
So he tied his shoe-lace.

2

And he packed every necessary thing.
Not much. But this and that into his bundle sped.
So the pipe that he smoked every evening,
And the slender book that he always read.
Also a ration of white bread.

3

Was glad once more of the valley, and put it out of mind
When towards the mountains he began to track.
And his ox was glad of all the new grass it could find,
Chewing, as it carried the old man on its back.
For he was not the hurrying kind.

4

But before the fourth day's rocky travelling was done,
A customs man interposed his authority.
'Please declare your valuables!' – 'None.'
And the boy who led the ox said: 'A teacher, you see.'
This met the contingency.

5

But the man, cheerful, and struck by a sudden notion,
Went on to ask: 'Who discovered something, you'd say?'
The boy replied: 'That yielding water in motion
Gets the better in the end of granite and porphyry.
You get me: the hard thing gives way.'

6

To lose no more time in the failing light
The boy drove on the ox, and the three had passed
Behind a black Scotch fir, and were out of sight
When our man, jerked into action at last,
Yelled out: 'Hey there, stop! Not so fast!

7

What's this about water, old man, that's so special?'
The old man stopped: 'Does it interest you?'
Said the other: 'I'm only a customs official,
But who gets the better of whom, that interests me too.
If you know and can tell me, do!

8

Write it down for me. Dictate it to this boy.
You don't take things like that with you. Have a care.
Of paper and ink we've a copious supply.
And there's a bite for you too: I live in there.
Well, do you call that fair?'

9

Over his shoulder the old sage now
Glanced at the man. Patched coat. Never owned a shoe.
One deep wrinkle his brow.
Oh, this was no victor. So much he knew.
And he murmured: 'You too?'

10

To reject a courteous suggestion
The old man, it seemed, was too old.

For he said aloud: 'Those who ask a question
Deserve an answer.' Said the boy: 'And it's turning cold.'
'We'll stay then. Hold!'

11

And the sage dismounted, having made his choice.
For seven days the two of them wrote on.
The customs man brought them food (and all that time lowered
                                                           his voice
When he swore at the smugglers and those on the run).
Then the work was done.

12

And one morning the boy could present to
The customs man eighty-one maxims completed,
And, thanking him for his gift of a small memento,
To the rocky track, round that fir, they retreated.
Rare politeness, you'll grant. Can you beat it?

13

But not to that wise man alone our praise is due
Whose name adorns the book *Tao Te Ching*.
For the wise man's wisdom must be dragged out of him too.
So the customs man also deserves our thanks for the thing:
He did the eliciting.

translated by Michael Hamburger

The poem offers an occasion to discuss the special role which the
quality of friendliness plays in the author's imagination. Brecht
allocates an important place to this quality. If we visualize the legend
he is telling, we see, on one side, the wisdom of Lao Tzu (who, by
the way, is not referred to by name) – a wisdom for which he is
about to pay with exile – and, on the other side, the customs official's desire for knowledge, for which at the end we are grateful
because it extracted the wise man's wisdom from him. But this
would never have happened without a third factor, and this factor
is *friendliness*. It might be untrue to say that friendliness is the actual

content of the book, *Tao Te Ching*; but it would be entirely true to say that, according to the legend, without the spirit of friendliness the book would never have been handed down to us. About this friendliness the poem has much to tell us.

First of all: friendliness is not dispensed without due forethought.

> *Over his shoulder the old sage now*
> *Glanced at the man. Patched coat. Never owned a shoe.*

Let the request be as courteous as it may, Lao Tzu first assures himself that the man who makes it is entitled to do so.

Secondly, friendliness does not consist in doing small things casually, but in doing the very greatest things as though they were the smallest. Once Lao Tzu has ascertained the customs official's right to ask, he places the next few days – those world-historic days during which, to please the other man, he interrupts his journey – under the motto:

> *'We'll stay then. Hold!'*

Thirdly, we learn about friendliness that it does not abolish the distance between human beings but brings that distance to life. After the wise man has done such a great thing *for* the customs official, he has little more to do *with* him, and it is not he but the boy who hands over the eighty-one maxims.

'The classics,' an old Chinese philosopher has said, 'lived in the darkest and bloodiest times and were the friendliest and most cheerful people that have ever been seen.' The Lao Tzu of this legend seems to spread cheerfulness wherever he goes. His ox, undeterred by the old man's weight on his back, is glad of all the green grass it can find. His boy is cheerful when, in order to explain Lao Tzu's poverty, he puts in dryly: 'A teacher, you see.' The customs official by his toll-gate is in a cheerful mood, and it is this cheerfulness that inspires him with the happy idea of asking for the results of Lao Tzu's research. Finally, how could the sage not be cheerful himself? At the first turning of the road he put out of his mind the valley which only a moment before had made him glad. What would his wisdom be worth if he could not also forget his anxiety about the future almost as soon as he felt it?

In the *Household Messenger* Brecht wrote a ballad about the friend-linesses of the world. They are three in number: the mother puts nap-kins on the child; the father takes the boy by the hand; people throw handfuls of earth on the man's grave. And that is enough. For at the end of the poem it is said:

> *Almost everyone has loved the world*
> *When he receives two handfuls of earth.*

The manifestations of the friendliness of the world are to be found at the hardest moments of existence: at birth, at the first step into life and at the last one, which leads out of life. That is the minimum programme of humanity. It recurs in the Lao Tzu poem in the form of the maxim:

> *'You get me: the hard thing gives way.'*

The poem comes to us at a time when such words ring in the ears of men like a promise which has nothing to concede to the promises of a Messiah. For the contemporary reader, however, they contain not only a promise but also a lesson.

> *' . . . That yielding water in motion*
> *Gets the better in the end of granite and porphyry.'*

The lesson or advice here is never to forget about the inconstancy and changeability of things, and to align oneself with those things which are inconspicuous and sober and inexhaustible, like water. The materialist dialectician will be reminded of the cause of the oppressed. (It is an inconspicuous thing for the rulers, a sober one for the oppressed and, in its consequences, the most inexhaustible of all.) Lastly, apart from the promise and the theory, there is a moral in the poem. Whoever wants to make the hard thing give way should miss no opportunity for friendliness.

BRECHT'S THREEPENNY NOVEL

Eight Years

Between the *Threepenny Opera* and the *Threepenny Novel* lies an interval of eight years. The new work developed out of the old. But this did not happen in the complex way in which one generally imagines the maturing of a work of art. These years were politically decisive. The author has assimilated their lessons; he has called the misdeeds that were perpetrated during those years by their true name, and lit a candle for their victims. He has written a satirical novel of major calibre.

To write this book he has begun again at the beginning. Little remains of the opera's basic elements or of its plot. Only the central characters are still the same. For it was they who, before our eyes, began to grow during those years and who so brutally claimed the space necessary for their growth. When the *Threepenny Opera* first appeared upon the German stage, the gangster was still a stranger there. In the meantime, he has made himself at home and has made barbarity a way of life. For the drastic, extreme quality which, at the very beginning of capitalism, characterizes the misery of the exploited, becomes manifest in the exploiters only at a late stage.

Brecht is concerned with both exploited and exploiters; that is why he telescopes different historical periods together and puts his gangster types down in a London which has the rhythm and outward look of Dickensian times. The conditions of private life are the old ones, those of the class struggle belong to our own time. These Londoners do not have the telephone, but their police is already equipped with tanks. The London of today – it has been said – demonstrates that it is good for capitalism to preserve a certain backwardness. Brecht has turned this circumstance to advantage. He peoples the stuffy offices, dank bathing establishments and foggy streets with types whose manners are often old-fashioned, but whose proceedings are always modern. Such displacements belong to the optic of the satire. Brecht underlines them with the licences he takes with London's topography. The behaviour of his characters, whom he has drawn from life, is – the satirist may say to himself – far more incredible than any Brobdingnag or London which he may have constructed inside his head.

Old Acquaintances

Those characters, then, appeared anew before their author. There is Peachum, who always keeps his hat on because there is no roof which he does not expect to collapse over his head. He has neglected his instrument shop for the sake of a wartime deal involving transport ships, where his army of beggars become useful, at critical moments, as an 'excited crowd'. The ships are to be used as troop transports in the Boer War. Being rotten, they go down with all hands not far from the Thames estuary. Peachum, who insists on attending the memorial service for the drowned sailors, hears, together with many others including a certain Fewkoombey, a bishop preaching a sermon on the biblical recommendation to practise usury with the talents (or pounds) one has received in trust. By this time Peachum has already insured himself against any serious consequences of the deal by eliminating his business associate. But he has not committed the murder himself. His daughter, 'the Peach', likewise becomes involved in criminal affairs, but only of a kind suitable for

a lady, i.e. a case of abortion and one of adultery. We are introduced
to the doctor she has chosen to perform the operation, and we hear
from his lips a discourse which is a counterpart to that delivered
by the bishop.

In the *Threepenny Opera* the hero, Macheath, had not yet gone
much beyond the years of his apprenticeship. The novel recapitu-
lates those years only briefly; it respects that 'semi-darkness which
obscures whole series of years . . . [and] makes the biographies of
our great businessmen so poor in material';* it offers no opinion on
whether or not the transformations by which the timber merchant
Beckett becomes the city man Macheath began with the murderer
Stanford Sills, known as 'The Knife'. All that is clear is that the
businessman remains loyal to certain friends from earlier times who
have not found their way into legality. This loyalty pays off inasmuch as such friends can procure by theft the large amounts of goods
which are then sold at unbeatably low prices in Macheath's chain-
stores.

Macheath's business is founded upon the B.shops, whose owners
(operating on an independent basis) have the sole obligation of
distributing his goods and paying rent for their shop premises. In a
newspaper interview Macheath speaks about 'his important discovery of the urge towards individual independence'. True, some of
these independent shopkeepers are in difficulties, and one of them –
a woman – actually drowns herself in the Thames because Macheath,
for business reasons, temporarily discontinues the supply of goods to
her shop. A suspicion of murder arises; there is a criminal case. But
this criminal case is absorbed in its entirety into the satirical design
of the novel. A society that looks for the murderer of a woman who
has committed suicide can never recognize him in Macheath, who
has merely exercised his contractual rights. 'The murder of the shop-
keeper Mary Sawyer' not only stands at the centre of the novel, but
also contains its moral. The petty shopkeepers who are gradually
bled white, the soldiers packed into unseaworthy ships, the burglars

* All quotations from *The Threepenny Novel* are taken from the Penguin
edition translated by Desmond Vesey (Harmondsworth, 1961; since reprinted)
(Translator's note).

whose boss has the chief of police in his pay – this grey mass, which in the novel occupies the place of the chorus in opera, supplies the rulers with their victims. On this mass they practise their crimes. To it belongs Mary Sawyer who is forced to drown herself, and from it comes Fewkoombey who, to his astonishment, is hanged for her murder.

A New Face

The soldier Fewkoombey, who in the prologue to the novel is assigned his 'abode' in a tin hut in Peachum's yard, and to whom, in the epilogue, 'the poor man's pound' is revealed in a dream, is a new face. Or rather, scarcely a new face but a 'transparent and face-less' one, like the face of the millions who fill the barracks and the tenement cellars. Placed hard by the picture frame, he is a life-size figure that points to the centre of the picture. He points at the crimi-nal bourgeois society in the middle ground. In that society he has the first word, for without him it would make no profits; that is why Fewkoombey appears in the prologue. And he appears as a judge in the epilogue because otherwise the criminal society would have the last word. Between the two there lies a short period of half a year, which he merely idles away, but during which certain affairs con-ducted by his superiors develop so favourably and on so wide a scale that the six months can end with Fewkoombey being hanged without the last-minute appearance of a 'king's messenger mounted on a horse'.

A little before this he has, as we have said, a dream. It is a dream about a court trial which concerns 'an especial crime'. ' . . . Because no one can stop a dreamer from getting what he wants, our friend became the judge of the greatest arraignment of all times, of the only really essential, comprehensive, and just tribunal that has ever existed. . . . After lengthy reflection, which itself lasted for months, the judge decided to start with a man who, according to a bishop's sermon at a memorial service for drowned soldiers, had invented a parable which had been used in pulpits for two thousand years. In the view of the supreme judge, this constituted an especial crime.'

The judge substantiates this view by naming the consequences of the parable and questioning a long row of witnesses who have to testify about *their* pound.

'Have you increased your pound?' asked the judge severely.
They shrank back in terror and said: 'No.'
'Did he [meaning the accused] see that your pound did not increase?'
At this question they did not at first know what they ought to answer. But after a time one of them stepped forward, a little boy. . . .
'He must have seen it; for we froze when it was cold, and we starved both before and after we had eaten. Look for yourself and see if we show it or not.'
He stuck two fingers into his mouth and whistled; and out . . . stepped a woman. And the woman was the living image of Mary Sawyer.

When, in the face of such damaging evidence, the accused is allowed a counsel for the defence – 'but he must be suited to you' – and Peachum presents himself in this role, the client's guilt becomes more clearly defined. He must be accused as an accessory: because, says the supreme judge, he gave people this parable, which is also a pound. Whereupon he condemns the accused to death. But the one that is actually hanged is the dreamer, who, in a lucid moment, understood how far back in history go the traces of the crimes of which he and his like are the victims.

Macheath's Party

In textbooks of criminal law, criminals are defined as anti-social elements. This may be true of the majority of criminals. In the case of some among them, however, history has proved the contrary. By turning many people into criminals they themselves became models of social behaviour. This is true of Macheath. He belongs to the new school, whilst his father-in-law, who is his equal and his enemy of long standing, still belongs to the old. Peachum is incapable of cutting a dash. He conceals his greed behind a sense of family, his impotence behind asceticism, his blackmailing activities behind charitable works. Best of all he likes to disappear into his office. The same cannot be said of Macheath. He is a born leader. His words are those of a statesman, his deeds those of a man of business. And indeed, the tasks he is called upon to perform are varied in the extreme. Never have they been more taxing for a leader of men than today. It is not enough to have recourse to violence for the preservation of property relations. It is not enough to stir up violence among the expropriated themselves. These are practical problems that have to be coped with. But just as a ballet dancer is required not only to be able to dance, but also to be pretty, so fascism not only demands a saviour of capital, but also that he be a man of outstanding moral worth. That is why a type like Macheath is so invaluable in our time.

He is an adept at displaying what the stunted petty bourgeois understands by a personality. Ruled by a hundred different authorities, the plaything of periodic price increases, the victim of crises, this cipher of statistics, this petty bourgeois looks for a man he can trust. No one wants to account to the petty bourgeois: but there is one who will. And he can. The dialectic at work is as follows: if this one man agrees to bear the responsibility, the petty bourgeois will show his gratitude by promising not to demand any kind of account from him. He will refuse to make any demands 'because that would show Mr Macheath that we have lost confidence in him'. The leader's leadership is the obverse of the petty bourgeois' contentedness. This contentedness never ceases to gratify Macheath. He misses no opportunity to take the centre of the stage. And he is a different man in front of the bankers, a different one in front of the owners of the B. shops, a different one before the court and a different one again before the members of his gang. He proves that 'one can say everything if only one has an unshakable will'. For example the following:

'In my opinion, which is the opinion of a hard-working business man, we haven't got the right men at the head of the country. They all belong to some party or other, and parties are, of necessity, self-seeking and egotistic. Their outlook is one-sided. We need men who stand above all parties, something like us business men. We sell our wares to rich and poor alike. Without regard for his standing, we are ready to sell any man a hundredweight of potatoes, to install electric light for him, to paint his house. The government of the state is a moral task. Everything must be so organized that the entrepreneur is a good entrepreneur, the worker a good worker,

in short, that the rich are good rich and the poor good poor. I am convinced that in time that form of government will come. And it will count
me among its supporters.'

Crude Thinking

Brecht has had Macheath's programme and many other reflections
set in italics, so that they stand out from the narrative text. In this
way he has created a collection of speeches and maxims, confessions
and pleas which can be described as unique. It alone would ensure
that the book will last. What is written here has never yet been expressed by anyone, and yet they all talk like this. The passages interrupt the text; they are – and in this they resemble illustrations – an
invitation to the reader to abandon illusion once in a while. Nothing
is more suitable for a satirical novel. Some of these passages cast a
strong light on the fundamental presuppositions to which Brecht
owes the force of his impact. In one of them we read, for example:
'The most important thing is to learn to think crudely. Crude thinking is the thinking of great men.'

There are many people to whom a dialectician means a lover of
subtleties. In this connection it is particularly useful when Brecht puts
his finger on 'crude thinking' which produces dialectics as its
opposite, contains it within itself, and has need of it. Crude thoughts
belong to the household of dialectical thinking precisely because
they represent nothing other than the application of theory to
practice: its *application* to practice, not its *dependence* on practice.
Action can, of course, be as subtle as thought. But a thought must
be crude in order to come into its own in action.

The forms of crude thinking change slowly, because they have
been created by the masses. Even those that are dead still contain a
lesson for us. One of these forms is the proverb, and the proverb is a
school of crude thinking. 'Has Mr Macheath got Mary Sawyer on
his conscience?' the people ask. Brecht presses their noses into the
answer by heading this chapter with the following proverb: 'There's
no smoke without fire.' Another chapter might have been headed:
'You can't make an omelette without breaking eggs.' It is the

chapter in which Peachum, the 'top authority in the matter of misery', considers the fundamentals of the begging business.

'It's plain to me now,' he says to himself, 'why people don't examine the injuries of beggars more closely before they give. They are convinced that the wounds are there, because they themselves have dealt them. When a man does business, isn't there another man somewhere else who is being ruined? When a man supports his family, aren't other families being forced into the gutter? All these people are already convinced that, because of their own way of living, there must be dirty, poverty-stricken wretches creeping about everywhere. Why, therefore, should they take the trouble to make sure of that? For the sake of the few pennies which they are willing to give?'

The Criminal Society

Peachum has grown in stature since the *Threepenny Opera*. His undeceivable eyes survey the triumphs of his successful speculations as well as the errors of his unsuccessful ones. No veil, not the smallest illusion conceals the laws of exploitation from his gaze. Such are this old-fashioned, solitary small man's credentials as a highly modern thinker. He is easily a match for Spengler, who has shown how useless the humanitarian and philanthropic ideologies dating from the beginnings of the bourgeois era have become for the entre-preneur today. The fact is that the accomplishments of technology are of benefit, first and foremost, to the ruling classes. This applies to progressive forms of thought as much as to modern forms of transport. The gentlemen in the *Threepenny Novel* do not have motor cars, it is true, but they are dialecticians to a man. Peachum, for example, says to himself that murderers are punished. 'But a non-murderer is also punished – and far more terribly. . . . An exist-ence in the slums, such as I and my family were threatened with, is nothing less than imprisonment. That is a life sentence!'

The detective novel which in its early days (in Dostoyevsky) did so much to advance psychology, has now, at the height of its devel-opment, become an instrument of social criticism. If Brecht's book exploits the genre more exhaustively than Dostoyevsky, one of the reasons is that in Brecht's book – as in real life – the criminal makes his living within society, and society – as in real life – takes its share of the spoils. Dostoyevsky was concerned with psychology; he revealed the criminal latent in man. Brecht is concerned with politics; he reveals the crime latent in business.

According to the rules of the detective novel, bourgeois legality and crime are two opposites. Brecht's procedure consists in retaining the highly developed technique of the detective novel but abandoning its rules. *This* detective novel depicts the objective truth about the relationship between bourgeois legality and crime, the latter being shown as a special case of exploitation sanctioned by the former. Sometimes one slides easily into the other. The thoughtful Peachum observes 'how the most complicated business is often put right by the simplest age-old methods. . . . All this business began with contracts and government stamps, and at the end we had to resort to murder! How I hate murder! . . . And to think that we were only doing business together!'

It is quite natural that in this borderline case of a detective novel there is no place for a detective. The role of agent of the law allotted to the detective under the rules of the game is here taken over by Competition. What takes place between Macheath and Peachum is a struggle between rival gangs, and the happy end is a gentlemen's agreement which formally apportions to each his share of the booty.

Satire and Marx

Brecht strips the conditions under which we live of their drapery of legal concepts. Their human content emerges from under them naked, as it will go down to posterity. Unfortunately, it has a dehumanized look. But that is not the satirist's fault. To lay bare his fellow citizen is his task. He may equip him with new clothes – may represent him, like Cervantes, in the form of the dog Berganza, like Swift in the equine form of the Houyhnhnms or, like Hoffmann, in the form of a cat – yet at heart he is concerned only with displaying the personage in a single posture: standing naked among his costumes. For the satirist, the nakedness with which he confronts his fellow citizen in a mirror is sufficient. His office goes no further than that.

Thus, Brecht contents himself with a slight change of costume for his contemporaries. This change of costume is just enough to create a continuity with the nineteenth century, the century which produced not only imperialism but also Marxism. And Marxism has some highly pertinent questions to put to imperialism. 'When the German Kaiser sent a telegram to President Kruger, whose shares rose then and whose fell?' 'Of course it's only the communists who ask that.' Marx, who was the first to illuminate with criticism the debased and mystified relations between men in capitalist society, thereby became a teacher of satire; and he was not far from becoming a master of it. It is with Marx that Brecht has gone to school. Satire, which has always been a materialist art, has with Brecht become a dialectical one. Marx stands in the background of his novel – more or less in the same way as Confucius and Zoroaster stood in the background of the mandarins and shahs who critically survey the French in the satires of the Enlightenment. Here, Marx determines the length of the distance which great writers generally, and great satirists in particular, must place between themselves and their subject matter. It has always been this distance that posterity makes its own when it calls an author 'classic'. We may suppose that posterity will easily find its way about in the *Threepenny Novel*.

*Il s'agit de gagner les intellectuels à la classe
ouvrière, en leur faisant prendre conscience
de l'identité de leurs démarches spirituelles et
de leurs conditions de producteur.*

[RAMON FERNANDEZ]

THE
AUTHOR
AS
PRODUCER*

You will remember how Plato, in his project for a
Republic, deals with writers. In the interests of the community,
he denies them the right to dwell therein. Plato had a high opinion
of the power of literature. But he thought it harmful and superflu-
ous – in a *perfect* community, be it understood. Since Plato, the
question of the writer's right to exist has not often been raised with
the same emphasis; today, however, it arises once more. Of course
it only seldom arises in this *form*. But all of you are more or less
conversant with it in a different form, that of the question of the
writer's autonomy: his freedom to write just what he pleases. You
are not inclined to grant him this autonomy. You believe that
the present social situation forces him to decide in whose service he
wishes to place his activity. The bourgeois author of entertainment
literature does not acknowledge this choice. You prove to him that,
without admitting it, he is working in the service of certain class
interests. A progressive type of writer does acknowledge this choice.
His decision is made upon the basis of the class struggle: he places
himself on the side of the proletariat. And that's the end of his

* Address delivered at the Institute for the Study of Fascism, Paris, on
27 April 1934.

autonomy. He directs his activity towards what will be useful to the proletariat in the class struggle. This is usually called pursuing a tendency, or 'commitment'.

Here you have the key word around which a debate has been going on for a long time. You are familiar with it, and so you know how unfruitful this debate has been. For the fact is that this debate has never got beyond a boring 'on-the-one-hand', 'on-the-other-hand': *on the one hand* one must demand the right tendency (or commitment) from a writer's work, *on the other hand* one is entitled to expect his work to be of a high quality. This formula is, of course, unsatisfactory so long as we have not understood the precise nature of the relationship which exists between the two factors, commitment and quality. One can declare that a work which exhibits the right tendency need show no further quality. Or one can decree that a work which exhibits the right tendency must, of necessity, show every other quality as well.

This second formulation is not without interest; more, it is correct. I make it my own. But in doing so I refuse to decree it. This assertion must be *proved*. And it is for my attempt to prove it that I now ask for your attention. – You may object that this is a rather special, indeed a far-fetched subject. You may ask whether I hope to advance the study of fascism with such a demonstration. – That is indeed my intention. For I hope to be able to show you that the concept of commitment, in the perfunctory form in which it generally occurs in the debate I have just mentioned, is a totally inadequate instrument of political literary criticism. I should like to demonstrate to you that the tendency of a work of literature can be politically correct only if it is also correct in the literary sense. That means that the tendency which is politically correct includes a literary tendency. And let me add at once: this literary tendency, which is implicitly or explicitly included in every correct political tendency, this and nothing else makes up the quality of a work. It is because of this that the correct political tendency of a work extends also to its literary quality: because a political tendency which is correct comprises a literary tendency which is correct.

I hope to be able to promise you that this assertion will presently become clearer. For the moment allow me to interject that I could have chosen a different point of departure for the considerations I wish to put before you. I began with the unfruitful debate concerning the relationship between the tendency and the quality of literary works. This argument is discredited, and rightly so. It is regarded as a textbook example of an attempt to deal with literary relationships undialectically, with stereotypes. But what if we treat the same problem dialectically?

For the dialectical treatment of this problem – and now I come to the heart of the matter – the rigid, isolated object (work, novel, book) is of no use whatsoever. It must be inserted into the context of living social relations. You rightly point out that this has been undertaken time and again in the circle of our friends. Certainly. But the discussion has often moved on directly to larger issues and therefore, of necessity, has often drifted into vagueness. Social relations, as we know, are determined by production relations. And when materialist criticism approached a work, it used to ask what was the position of that work *vis-à-vis* the social production relations of its time. That is an important question. But also a very difficult one. The answer to it is not always unequivocal. And I should now like to propose a more immediate question for your consideration. A question which is somewhat more modest, which goes less far, but which, it seems to me, stands a better chance of being answered. Instead of asking: what is the position of a work *vis-à-vis* the productive relations of its time, does it underwrite these relations, is it reactionary, or does it aspire to overthrow them, is it revolutionary? – instead of this question, or at any rate before this question, I should like to propose a different one. Before I ask: what is a work's position *vis-à-vis* the production relations of its time, I should like to ask: what is its position *within* them? This question concerns the function of a work within the literary production relations of its time. In other words, it is directly concerned with literary *technique*.

By mentioning technique I have named the concept which makes literary products accessible to immediate social, and therefore materialist, analysis. At the same time, the concept of technique represents the dialectical starting-point from which the sterile dichotomy of form and content can be surmounted. And furthermore this concept of technique contains within itself an indication of the right way to determine the relationship between tendency and quality, which was the object of our original inquiry. If, then, we were entitled earlier on to say that the correct political tendency of a work includes its literary quality because it includes its literary tendency, we can now affirm more precisely that this literary tendency may consist in a progressive development of literary technique, or in a regressive one.

It will surely meet with your approval if, at this point, and with only apparent inconsequence, I turn to a set of entirely concrete literary relations: those of Russia. I should like to guide your attention to Sergey Tretyakov and to the type of 'operative' writer he defines and personifies. This operative writer offers the most palpable example of the functional dependency which always and in all circumstances exists between the correct political tendency and a progressive literary technique. Admittedly it is only one example; I reserve the right to quote others later on. Tretyakov distinguishes between the operative and the informative writer. The operative writer's mission is not to report but to fight; not to assume the spectator's role but to intervene actively. He defines this mission with the data he supplies about his own activity. When, in 1928, in the period of total collectivization of Russian agriculture, the slogan 'Writers to the Collective Farm!' was issued, Tretyakov went to the 'Communist Lighthouse' commune and, in the course of two prolonged visits, understood the following activities: calling mass meetings; collecting funds for down-payments on tractors; persuading private farmers to join the collective farm; inspecting reading-rooms; launching wall newspapers and directing the collective farm newspaper; reporting to Moscow newspapers; introducing radio, travelling film shows, etc. It is not surprising that the book *Feld-Herren* ('Field Commanders') which Tretyakov wrote following these visits is said to have exercised considerable influence on the subsequent organizing of collective farms.

You may admire Tretyakov and yet think that his example is not particularly meaningful in this connection. The tasks he undertook, you may object, are those of a journalist or propagandist; all this has not much to do with literary creation. Yet I quoted Tretyakov's example deliberately in order to point out to you how wide the horizon has to be from which, in the light of the technical realities of our situation today, we must rethink the notions of literary forms or genres if we are to find forms appropriate to the literary energy of our time. Novels did not always exist in the past, nor must they necessarily always exist in the future; nor, always, tragedies; nor great epics; literary forms such as the commentary, the translation, yes, even the pastiche, have not always existed merely as minor exercises in the margin of literature, but have had a place, not only in the philosophical but also the literary traditions of Arabia or China. Rhetoric was not always a trifling form; on the contrary, it left an important mark on large areas of ancient literature. All this to familiarize you with the idea that we are in the midst of a vast process in which literary forms are being melted down, a process in which many of the contrasts in terms of which we have been accustomed to think may lose their relevance. Let me give an example of the unfruitfulness of such contrasts and of the process of their dialectical resolution. This will bring us once more to Tretyakov. For my example is the newspaper.

'In our literature,' writes an author of the Left,* 'contrasts which, in happier epochs, used to fertilize one another have become insoluble antinomies. Thus, science and *belles lettres*, criticism and original production, culture and politics now stand apart from one another without connection or order of any kind. The newspaper is the arena of this literary confusion. Its content eludes any form of organization other than that which is imposed upon it by the reader's impatience. And this impatience is not just the impatience of the politician waiting for information or that of the speculator waiting for a tip-off: behind it smoulders the impatience of the outsider, the excluded man who yet believes he has a right to speak out in his own interest. The editorial offices have long ago learned to exploit the fact that nothing binds the reader to his newspaper so much as this

* Benjamin himself: cf. *Schriften*, Frankfurt, 1955, vol. 1, p. 384.

impatience, which demands fresh nourishment every day; they exploit it by continually throwing open new columns for readers' questions, opinions and protests. Thus the unselective assimilation of facts goes hand in hand with an equally unselective assimilation of readers, who see themselves elevated instantaneously to the rank of correspondents. There is however a dialectical factor hidden in this situation: the decline of literature in the bourgeois press is proving to be the formula for its regeneration in the Soviet press. For as literature gains in breadth what it loses in depth, so the distinction between author and public, which the bourgeois press maintains by artificial means, is beginning to disappear in the Soviet press. The reader is always prepared to become a writer, in the sense of being one who describes or prescribes.* As an expert – not in any particular trade, perhaps, but anyway an expert on the subject of the job he happens to be in – he gains access to authorship. Work itself puts in a word. And writing about work makes up part of the skill necessary to perform it. Authority to write is no longer founded in a specialist training but in a polytechnical one, and so becomes common property. In a word, the literarization of living conditions becomes a way of surmounting otherwise insoluble antinomies, and the place where the words is most debased – that is to say, the newspaper – becomes the very place where a rescue operation can be mounted.'

I hope to have shown by the foregoing that the view of the author as producer must go all the way back to the press. Through the example of the press, at any rate the Soviet Russian press, we see that the vast melting-down process of which I spoke not only destroys the conventional separation between genres, between writer and poet, scholar and popularizer, but that it questions even the separation between author and reader. The press is the most decisive point of reference for this process, and that is why any consideration of the author as producer must extend to and include the press.

But it cannot stop there. For, as we know, the newspaper in

* Benjamin makes a play on words here with *Schreibender* (one who writes), *Beschreibender* (one who describes) and *Vorschreibender* (one who prescribes) (Translator's note).

Western Europe does not yet represent a valid instrument of production in the writer's hands. It still belongs to capital. Since, on the one hand, the newspaper is, technically speaking, the writer's most important strategic position, and since, on the other hand, this position is in the hands of the enemy, it should not surprise us if the writer's attempt to understand his socially conditioned nature, his technical means and his political task runs into the most tremendous difficulties. One of the decisive developments in Germany during the last ten years was that many of her productive minds, under the pressure of economic circumstances, underwent a revolutionary development in terms of their *mentality* – without at the same time being able to think through in a really revolutionary way the question of their own work, its relationship to the means of production and its technique. As you see, I am speaking of the so-called left intelligentsia and in so doing I propose to confine myself to the bourgeois left intelligentsia which, in Germany, has been at the centre of the important literary-political movements of the last decade. I wish to single out two of these movements, Activism and New Objectivity (*Neue Sachlichkeit*), in order to show by their example that political commitment, however revolutionary it may seem, functions in a counter-revolutionary way so long as the writer experiences his solidarity with the proletariat only *in the mind* and not as a producer.

The slogan which sums up the claims of the Activist group is 'logocracy', or, translated into the vernacular, the sovereignty of mind. This is apt to be understood as the rule of 'men of mind', or intellectuals; indeed, the notion of 'men of mind' has become accepted by the left-wing intelligentsia and dominates their political manifestos, from Heinrich Mann to Döblin. Quite obviously this notion was coined without any regard to the position of the intelligentsia in the production process. Hiller himself, the theoretician of Activism, does not want the notion of 'men of mind' to be understood to mean 'members of certain professions' but as 'representatives of a certain characterological type'. Naturally, this characterological type occupies, as such, a position between the classes. It includes any number of private persons without offering the smallest basis for their organization into a collective. When Hiller formulates his rejection of the various Party leaders, he concedes that they may have many advantages over him; they may 'have more knowledge of important things . . . speak the language of the people better . . . fight more courageously' than he, but of one thing he is certain: 'their thinking is more faulty'. I daresay it is; but what is the use of that if the important thing in politics is not private thinking but, as Brecht once put it, the art of thinking inside other people's heads?* Activism tried to replace materialist dialectics by the value, undefinable in class terms, of ordinary common sense. At best, its 'men of mind' represent a certain attitude. In other words: the principle upon which this collective is based is in itself a reactionary one; no wonder then that the effect of the collective was never revolutionary.

The pernicious principle behind such a method of forming a collective continues, however, to operate. We saw it at work when Döblin published his *Wissen und Verändern* ('To Know and to Change') three years ago. This text, as we all remember, took the form of a reply to a young man – Döblin calls him Herr Hocke – who had addressed himself to the famous author with the question: 'What is to be done?' Döblin invites Herr Hocke to espouse the cause of Socialism, but on certain questionable conditions. Socialism, according to Döblin, is 'freedom, spontaneous association of human beings, refusal of all constraint, revolt against injustice and constraint; it is humanity, tolerance and peaceful intentions'. Be that as it may, he takes this socialism as the starting-point for an all-out attack upon the theory and practice of the radical working-class movement. 'Nothing,' writes Döblin, 'can develop out of another thing unless it is already present in it: out of murderously exacerbated class struggle may come justice, but not socialism.' 'You, my dear sir,' – this is how Döblin formulates the advice which, for this and other reasons, he offers to Herr Hocke – 'cannot, by joining the

---

* The following passage, later deleted, originally appeared in the manuscript in place of the next sentence: 'Or, in Trotsky's words: "When enlightened pacifists undertake to abolish War by means of rationalist arguments, they are simply ridiculous. When the armed masses start to take up the arguments of Reason against War, however, this signifies the end of war."'

proletarian front, give practical effect to the affirmation with which you respond in principle to the struggle (of the proletariat). You must confine yourself to approving this struggle with emotion and with sorrow; for you must know that, if you do more, then a tremendously important position will fall vacant . . . the original communist position of individual human freedom, of spontaneous solidarity and unity among men. . . . This, my dear Sir, is the only position appropriate to you.' Here it becomes palpably clear where the concept of the 'man of mind' as a type defined according to his opinions, intentions or predispositions, but not according to his position within the production process, must lead. This man, says Döblin, should find his place *at the side* of the proletariat. But what sort of a place is that? The place of a well-wisher, an ideological patron. An impossible place. And so we come back to the thesis we proposed at the beginning: the place of the intellectual in the class struggle can only be determined, or better still chosen, on the basis of his position within the production process.

Brecht has coined the phrase 'functional transformation' (*Umfunktionierung*) to describe the transformation of forms and instruments of production by a progressive intelligentsia – an intelligentsia interested in liberating the means of production and hence active in the class struggle. He was the first to address to the intellectuals the far-reaching demand that they should not supply the production apparatus without, at the same time, within the limits of the possible, changing that apparatus in the direction of Socialism. 'The publication of the *Versuche*,' we read in the author's introduction to the series of texts published under that title, 'marks a point at which certain works are not so much intended to represent individual experiences (i.e. to have the character of finished works) as they are aimed at using (transforming) certain existing institutes and institutions.' It is not spiritual renewal, as the fascists proclaim it, that is desirable; what is proposed is technical innovation. I shall return to this subject later. Here I should like to confine myself to pointing out the decisive difference between merely supplying a production apparatus and changing it. I should like to preface my remarks on the New Objectivity with the proposition that to supply a production apparatus without trying, within the limits of the possible, to change it, is a highly disputable activity even when the material supplied appears to be of a revolutionary nature. For we are confronted with the fact – of which there has been no shortage of proof in Germany over the last decade – that the bourgeois apparatus of production and publication is capable of assimilating, indeed of propagating, an astonishing amount of revolutionary themes without ever seriously putting into question its own continued existence or that of the class which owns it. In any case this remains true so long as it is supplied by hacks, albeit revolutionary hacks. And I define a hack as a man who refuses as a matter of principle to improve the production apparatus and so prise it away from the ruling class for the benefit of Socialism. I further maintain that an appreciable part of so-called left-wing literature had no other social function than that of continually extracting new effects or sensations from this situation for the public's entertainment. Which brings me to the New Objectivity. It launched the fashion for reportage. Let us ask ourselves whose interests were advanced by this technique.

For greater clarity let me concentrate on photographic reportage. Whatever applies to it is transferable to the literary form. Both owe their extraordinary development to publication techniques – radio and the illustrated press. Let us think back to Dadaism. The revolutionary strength of Dadaism lay in testing art for its authenticity. You made still-lifes out of tickets, spools of cotton, cigarette stubs, and mixed them with pictorial elements. You put a frame round the whole thing. And in this way you said to the public: look, your picture frame destroys time; the smallest authentic fragment of everyday life says more than painting. Just as a murderer's bloody fingerprint on a page says more than the words printed on it. Much of this revolutionary attitude passed into photomontage. You need only think of the works of John Heartfield, whose technique made the book jacket into a political instrument. But now let us follow the subsequent development of photography. What do we see? It has become more and more subtle, more and more modern, and the result is that it is now incapable of photographing a tenement or a rubbish-heap without transfiguring it. Not to mention a river dam or an electric cable factory: in front of these, photography can now only say, 'How beautiful.' *The World Is Beautiful* – that is the title of the well-known picture book by Renger-Patzsch in which we see New Objectivity photography at its peak. It has succeeded in turning abject poverty itself, by handling it in a modish, technically perfect way, into an object of enjoyment. For if it is an economic function of photography to supply the masses, by modish processing, with matter which previously eluded mass consumption – Spring, famous people, foreign countries – then one of its political functions is to renovate the world as it is from the inside, i.e. by modish techniques.

Here we have an extreme example of what it means to supply a production apparatus without changing it. Changing it would have meant bringing down one of the barriers, surmounting one of the contradictions which inhibit the productive capacity of the intelligentsia. What we must demand from the photographer is the ability to put such a caption beneath his picture as will rescue it from the ravages of modishness and confer upon it a revolutionary use value. And we shall lend greater emphasis to this demand if we, as writers, start taking photographs ourselves. Here again, therefore, technical progress is, for the author as producer, the basis of his political progress. In other words, intellectual production cannot become politically useful until the separate spheres of competence to which, according to the bourgeois view, the process of intellectual production owes its order, have been surmounted; more precisely, the barriers of competence must be broken down by each of the productive forces they were created to separate, acting in concert. By experiencing his solidarity with the proletariat, the author as producer experiences, directly and simultaneously, his solidarity with certain other producers who, until then, meant little to him.

I spoke of the photographer; let me now, very briefly, quote a remark of Hanns Eisler's about the musician: 'In the development of music, both in production and in reproduction, we must learn to recognize an ever-increasing process of rationalization. . . . The gramophone record, the sound film, the nickelodeon can . . . market the world's best musical productions in canned form. The consequence of this process of rationalization is that musical reproduction is becoming limited to groups of specialists which are getting smaller, but also more highly qualified, all the time. The crisis of concert-hall music is the crisis of a form of production made obsolete and overtaken by new technical inventions.' In other words, the task consisted in the 'functional transformation' of the concert-hall form of music in a manner which had to meet two conditions: that of removing, first, the dichotomy of performer and audience and, secondly, that of technical method and content. On this point Eisler makes the following interesting observation: 'We should beware of overestimating orchestral music and thinking of it as the only high art-form. Music without words acquired its great importance and its full development only under capitalism.' This suggests that the task of transforming concert music requires help from the word. Only such help can, as Eisler puts it, transform a concert into a political meeting. The fact that such a transformation may really represent a peak achievement of both musical and literary technique – this Brecht and Eisler have proved with their didactic play *The Measures Taken*.

If, at this point, you look back at the melting-down of literary forms of which we spoke earlier, you will see how photography and music join the incandescent liquid mass from which the new forms will be cast; and you will ask yourselves what other elements may likewise enter into it. Only the literarization of all living conditions gives some idea of the scope of this melting-down process; and the temperature at which the melting-down takes place (perfectly or imperfectly) is determined by the state of the class struggle.

I have spoken of the way in which certain modish photographers proceed in order to make human misery an object of consumption. Turning to the New Objectivity as a literary movement, I must go a step further and say that it has turned *the struggle against misery* into an object of consumption. In many cases, indeed, its political significance has been limited to converting revolutionary reflexes, in so far as these occurred within the bourgeoisie, into themes of entertainment and amusement which can be fitted without much difficulty into the cabaret life of a large city. The characteristic feature of this literature is the way it transforms political struggle so that it ceases to be a compelling motive for decision and becomes an object of comfortable contemplation; it ceases to be a means of production and becomes an article of consumption. A perceptive critic* has commented on this phenomenon, using Erich Kästner as an example, in the following terms: 'This left-radical intelligentsia has nothing to do with the working-class movement. It is a phenomenon of bourgeois decadence and as such the counterpart of that mimicry of feudalism which, in the Kaiser's time, was admired in a reserve lieutenant. Left-radical journalists of Kästner's, Tucholsky's or Mehring's type are a mimicry of the proletarian for decadent strata of the bourgeoisie. Their function, viewed politically, is to bring forth not parties but cliques; viewed from the literary angle, not schools but fashions; viewed economically, not producers but agents. Agents or hacks who make a great display of their poverty and turn the gaping void into a feast. One couldn't be more comfortable in an uncomfortable situation.'

This school, as I said, made a great display of its poverty. By so doing it evaded the most urgent task of the writer of today: that of recognizing how poor he is and how poor he must be in order to be able to begin again at the beginning. For that is the point at issue. True, the Soviet State does not, like Plato's Republic, propose to expel its writers, but it does – and this is why I mentioned Plato at the beginning – propose to assign to them tasks which will make it impossible for them to parade the richness of the creative personality, which has long been a myth and a fake, in new masterpieces. To expect a renovation – in the sense of more personalities and more works of this kind – is a privilege of fascism, which, in this context, produces such foolish formulations as the one with which Günther Gründel rounds off the literary section of *The Mission of the Young Generation*: 'We cannot close this . . . review of the present and outlook into the future . . . in a better way than by saying that the *Wilhelm Meister*, the *Grüne Heinrich* of our generation have not yet been written.' Nothing will be further from the mind of an author

* Cf. Walter Benjamin, 'Linke Melancholie' ('Left Melancholy'), on Erich Kästner's new book of poems, in *Die Gesellschaft*, 8 (1931), vol. I. pp. 182f. In quoting from himself, Benjamin has altered the original text.

who has carefully thought about the conditions of production today than to expect or even to want such works to be written. He will never be concerned with products alone, but always, at the same time, with the means of production. In other words, his products must possess an organizing function besides and before their character as finished works. And their organizational usefulness must on no account be confined to propagandistic use. Commitment alone will not do it. The excellent Lichtenberg said: 'It is not what a man is convinced of that matters, but what his convictions make of him.' Of course opinions matter quite a lot, but the best opinion is of no use if it does not make something useful of those who hold it. The best 'tendency' is wrong if it does not prescribe the attitude with which it ought to be pursued. And the writer can only prescribe such an attitude in the place where he is active, that is to say in his writing. Commitment is a necessary, but never a sufficient, condition for a writer's work acquiring an organizing function. For this to happen it is also necessary for the writer to have a teacher's attitude. And today this is more than ever an essential demand. *A writer who does not teach other writers teaches nobody*. The crucial point, therefore, is that a writer's production must have the character of a model: it must be able to instruct other writers in their production and, secondly, it must be able to place an improved apparatus at their disposal. This apparatus will be the better, the more consumers it brings in contact with the production process – in short, the more readers or spectators it turns into collaborators. We already possess a model of this kind, of which, however, I cannot speak here in any detail. It is Brecht's epic theatre.

Tragedies and operas are being written all the time, apparently with a trusty stage apparatus to hand, whereas in reality they do nothing but supply an apparatus which is obsolete. 'This confusion among musicians, writers and critics about their situation,' says Brecht, 'has enormous consequences, which receive far too little attention. Believing themselves to be in possession of an apparatus which in reality possesses them, they defend an apparatus over which they no longer have control, which is no longer, as they still believe, a means *for* the producers but has become a means to be used *against* the producers.' This theatre of complex machineries, gigantic armies of stage extras and extra-refined stage effects has become a means to be used against the producers, not least by the fact that it is attempting to recruit them in the hopeless competitive struggle forced upon it by film and radio. This theatre – it matters little whether we think of the theatre of culture or that of entertainment, since both are complementary to one another – is the theatre of a saturated stratum for which anything that comes its way is a stimulant. Its position is a lost one. Not so the position of a theatre which, instead of competing against the newer means of communication, tries to apply them and to learn from them – in short, to enter into a dialogue with them. This dialogue the epic theatre has adopted as its cause. Matching the present development of film and radio, it is the theatre for our time.

In the interests of this dialogue Brecht went back to the most fundamental and original elements of theatre. He confined himself, as it were, to a podium, a platform. He renounced plots requiring a great deal of space. Thus he succeeded in altering the functional relationship between stage and audience, text and production, producer and actor. Epic theatre, he declared, must not develop actions but represent conditions. As we shall presently see, it obtains its 'conditions' by allowing the actions to be interrupted. Let me remind of you of the 'songs', whose principal function consists in interrupting the action. Here, then – that is to say, with the principle of interruption – the epic theatre adopts a technique which has become familiar to you in recent years through film and radio, photography and the press. I speak of the technique of montage, for montage interrupts the context into which it is inserted. Allow me, however, to explain very briefly why it is here that this technique enjoys special, and perhaps supreme, rights.

The interrupting of the action, the technique which entitles Brecht to describe his theatre as *epic*, always works against creating an illusion among the audience. Such illusion is of no use to a theatre which proposes to treat elements of reality as if they were elements of an experimental set-up. Yet the conditions stand at the end, not the beginning of the test. These conditions are, in one form or another, the conditions of our life. Yet they are not brought close to the spectator; they are distanced from him. He recognizes them as real – not, as in the theatre of naturalism, with complacency, but with astonishment. Epic theatre does not reproduce conditions; rather, it discloses, it uncovers them. This uncovering of the conditions is effected by interrupting the dramatic processes; but such interruption does not act as a stimulant; it has an organizing function. It brings the action to a standstill in mid-course and thereby compels the spectator to take up a position towards the action, and the actor to take up a position towards his part. Let me give an example to show how Brecht, in his selection and treatment of gestures, simply uses the method of montage – which is so essential to radio and film – in such a way that it ceases to be a modish technique and becomes a human event. Picture to yourself a family row: the wife is just about to pick up a bronze statuette and hurl it at the daughter; the father is opening a window to call for help. At this moment a stranger enters. The process is interrupted; what becomes apparent in its place is the condition now exposed before the stranger's view: disturbed faces, open window, a devastated interior. There exists, however, a viewpoint from which even the more normal scenes of present-day life do not look so very different from this. That is the viewpoint of the epic dramatist.

He opposes the dramatic laboratory to the finished work of art. He goes back, in a new way, to the theatre's greatest and most ancient opportunity: the opportunity to expose the present. At the centre of his experiments stands man. The man of today; a reduced man, therefore, a man kept on ice in a cold world. But since he is the only one we've got, it is in our interest to know him. We subject him to tests and observations. The outcome is this: events are not changeable at their climax, not through virtue and resolve, but only in their strictly ordinary, habitual course, through reason and practice. The purpose of epic theatre is to construct out of the smallest elements of behaviour what Aristotelian drama calls 'action'. Its means, therefore, are more modest than those of traditional theatre; its aims likewise. It sets out, not so much to fill the audience with feelings – albeit possibly feelings of revolt – as to alienate the audience in a lasting manner, through thought, from the conditions in which it lives. Let me remark, by the way, that there is no better starting point for thought than laughter; speaking more precisely, spasms of the diaphragm generally offer better chances for thought than spasms of the soul. Epic theatre is lavish only in the occasions it offers for laughter.

You may have noticed that the reflections whose conclusions we are now nearing make only one demand on the writer: the demand to *think*, to reflect upon his position in the production process. We can be sure that such thinking, *in the writers who matter* – that is to say the best technicians in their particular branches of the trade – will sooner or later lead them to confirm very soberly their solidarity with the proletariat. To conclude, I should like to quote a topical proof of this in the form of a short passage from the Paris periodical *Commune*. This periodical held an inquiry under the title: 'For whom do you write?' I shall quote from the reply by René Maublanc and then some relevant comments by Aragon. Maublanc says: 'There is no doubt that I write almost exclusively for a bourgeois public. First, because I am obliged to [here he refers to his professional duties as a grammar-school teacher], and secondly because I am of bourgeois origin, had a bourgeois education, and come from a bourgeois environment and therefore am naturally inclined to address the class to which I belong, which I know best and can best understand. But that does not mean that I write to please that class or to uphold it. On the one hand, I am convinced that the proletarian revolution is necessary and desirable; on the other hand, I believe that the weaker the resistance of the bourgeoisie, the more rapid, the easier, the more successful and the less bloody this revolution will be. ... The proletariat today needs allies in the bourgeois camp, just as in the eighteenth century the bourgeoisie needed allies in the feudal camp. I should like to be among those allies.'

Aragon's comment on this is as follows: 'Our comrade here touches upon a state of affairs which affects a very large number of present-day writers. Not all have the courage to look it straight in the eye. ... Those who are as clear about their own position as René

Maublanc are rare. But it is precisely from these that we must demand still more. . . . It is not enough to weaken the bourgeoisie
from within: it is necessary to fight it *together with* the proletariat. . . .
René Maublanc and many of our friends among writers who are
still hesitant have before them the example of Soviet Russian writers
who came from the Russian bourgeoisie and yet became pioneers
of Socialist construction.'

Thus far Aragon. But how did these writers become pioneers?
Surely not without very bitter struggles and agonizing conflicts.
The considerations I put before you are an attempt to draw a positive balance from these struggles. They are founded upon the concept to which the debate concerning the attitude of Russian intellectuals owes its solution: the concept of the expert. The solidarity
of the expert with the proletariat – and therein lies the beginning
of this solution – can never be other than mediated. The Activists
and adherents of New Objectivity may strike whatever poses they
like, they can do nothing about the fact that even the proletarianization of the intellectual hardly ever makes him a proletarian. Why?
Because the bourgeois class has endowed him with a means of production – in the form of his education – which, on the grounds of
educational privilege, creates a bond of solidarity which attaches
him to his class, and still more attaches his class to him. Aragon was
therefore perfectly right when, in another context, he said: 'The
revolutionary intellectual appears first of all and above everything
else as a traitor to his class of origin.' In a writer this betrayal consists in an attitude which transforms him, from a supplier of the production apparatus, into an engineer who sees his task in adapting
that apparatus to the ends of the proletarian revolution. That is a
mediating effectiveness, but it nevertheless frees the intellectual
from the purely destructive task to which Maublanc, and many comrades with him, believe he has to be consigned. Will he succeed in
furthering the unification of the means of intellectual production?
Does he see ways of organizing the intellectual workers within their
actual production process? Has he suggestions for changing the
function of the novel, of drama, of poetry? The more completely
he can address himself to these tasks, the more correct his thinking

will be and, necessarily, the higher will be the technical quality of his work. And conversely: the more precisely he thus understands his own position within the production process, the less it will occur to him to pass himself off as a 'man of mind'. The mind, the spirit that makes itself heard in the name of fascism, *must* disappear. The mind which believes only in its own magic strength *will* disappear. For the revolutionary struggle is not fought between capitalism and mind. It is fought between capitalism and the proletariat.

CONVERSATIONS WITH BRECHT

1934

4 July. Yesterday, a long conversation in Brecht's sickroom about my essay 'The Author as Producer'. Brecht thought the theory I develop in the essay – that the attainment of technical progress in literature eventually changes the function of art forms (hence also of the intellectual means of production) and is therefore a criterion for judging the revolutionary function of literary works – applies to artists of only one type, the writers of the upper bourgeoisie, among whom he counts himself. 'For such a writer,' he said, 'there really exists a point of solidarity with the interests of the proletariat: it is the point at which he can develop his own means of production. Because he identifies with the proletariat at this point, he is proletarianized – completely so – at this same point, i.e. as a producer. And his complete proletarianization at this one point establishes his solidarity with the proletariat all along the line.' He thought my critique of proletarian writers of Becher's type too abstract, and tried to improve upon it by analysing a poem of Becher's which appeared in a recent issue of one of the proletarian literary reviews under the title *'Ich sage ganz offen'* ('I say quite openly'). Brecht compared this poem, first, with his own didactic poem about Carola Neher, the actress, and secondly with Rimbaud's *Bateau Ivre*. 'I taught Carola Neher all kinds of things, you know,' he said, 'not just acting – for example, she learned from me how to wash herself. Before that she used to wash just so as not to be dirty. But that was absolutely out of the question, you understand. So I taught her how to wash her face. She became so perfect at it that I wanted to film her doing it, but it never came to that because I didn't feel like doing any filming just then and she didn't feel like doing it in front of anybody else. That didactic poem was a model. Anyone who learned from it was supposed to put himself in place of the "I" of the poem. When Becher says "I", he considers himself – as president of the Union of German Proletarian-Revolutionary Writers – to be exemplary. The only trouble is that nobody feels like following his example. He gets nothing across except that he is rather pleased with himself.' In this connection Brecht said he has been meaning for a long time to write a series of such model poems for different trades – the engineer, the writer. Then he compared Becher's poem with Rimbaud's. He thinks that Marx and Engels themselves, had they read *Le Bateau Ivre*, would have sensed in it the great historical movement of which it is the expression. They would have clearly recognized that what it describes is not an eccentric poet going for a walk but the flight, the escape of a man who cannot bear to live any longer inside the barriers of a class which – with the Crimean War, with the Mexican adventure – was then beginning to open up even the more exotic continents to its mercantile interests. Brecht thinks it is impossible to turn Rimbaud's attitude – the attitude of the foot-loose vagabond who puts himself at the mercy of chance and turns his back upon society – into a model representation of a proletarian fighter.

6 July. Brecht, in the course of yesterday's conversation: 'I often imagine being interrogated by a tribunal. "Now tell us, Mr Brecht, are you really in earnest?" I would have to admit that no, I'm not completely in earnest. I think too much about artistic problems, you know, about what is good for the theatre, to be completely in earnest. But having said "no" to that important question, I would add something still more important: namely, that my attitude is, *permissible.*' I must admit he said this after the conversation had been going on for some little time. He started by expressing doubt, not as to whether his attitude was permissible, but whether it was effective. His first remark was in answer to something I had said about Gerhart Hauptmann. 'I sometimes ask myself,' he said, 'whether writers like Hauptmann aren't, after all, the only ones who really get anywhere: I mean the *substance writers* [*Substanz-Dichter*].' By this he means those writers who really are completely in earnest. To explain this thought he proceeds from the hypothesis that Confucius might once have written a tragedy, or Lenin a novel. That, he thinks, would be felt as improper, unworthy behaviour. 'Suppose you read a very good historical novel and later you discover that it is by Lenin. You would change your opinion of both, to the detriment of both. Likewise it would be wrong for Confucius to have written a tragedy, say one of Euripides's tragedies; it would be felt as unworthy. Yet his parables are not.' All this leads, in short, to a differentiation between two literary types: the visionary artist, who is in earnest, and the cool-headed thinking man, who is not completely in earnest. At this point I raised the question of Kafka. To which of the two groups does he belong? I know that the question cannot be answered. And it is precisely its unanswerability which Brecht regards as an indication of the fact that Kafka, whom he considers to be a great writer, is, like Kleist, Grabbe or Büchner, a failure. Kafka's starting point is really the parable, which is governed by reason and which, therefore, so far as its actual wording is concerned, cannot be entirely in earnest. But then this parable is, all the same, subjected to the process of form-giving. It grows into a novel. And if you look closely you see that it contained the germ of a novel from the start. It was never altogether transparent. I should add that Brecht is convinced that Kafka would not have found his own special form without Dostoyevsky's Grand Inquisitor or that other passage in *The Brothers Karamazov* where the holy *starets* begins to stink. In Kafka, then, the parabolic element is in conflict with the visionary element. But Kafka as a visionary, says Brecht, saw what was coming without seeing what *is*. He emphasizes once more (as earlier at Le Lavandou, but in terms which are clearer to me) the prophetic aspect of Kafka's work. Kafka had one problem and one only, he says, and that was the problem of organization. He was terrified by the thought of the empire of ants: the thought of men being alienated from themselves by the forms of their life in society. And he anticipated certain forms of this alienation, e.g. the methods of the GPU. But he never found a solution and never awoke from his nightmare. Brecht says of Kafka's precision that it is the precision of an imprecise man, a dreamer.

12 July. Yesterday after playing chess Brecht said: 'You know, when Korsch comes, we really ought to work out a new game with him. A game in which the moves do not always stay the same; where the function of every piece changes after it has stood in the same square for a while: it should either become stronger or weaker. This way the game doesn't develop, it stays the same for too long.'

23 July. Yesterday a visit from Karin Michaelis, who has just returned from her trip to Russia and is full of enthusiasm. Brecht remembers how he was taken round Moscow by Tretyakov. Tretyakov showed him the city and was proud of everything, no matter what it was. 'That isn't a bad thing,' says Brecht, 'it shows that the place belongs to him. One isn't proud of other people's property.' After a while he added; 'Yes, but in the end I got a bit tired of it. I couldn't admire everything, nor did I want to. The point is, they were his soldiers, his lorries. But not, alas, mine.'

24 July. On a beam which supports the ceiling of Brecht's study are painted the words: 'Truth is concrete.' On a window-sill stands a small wooden donkey which can nod its head. Brecht has hung a little sign round its neck on which he has written: 'Even I must understand it.'

5 August. Three weeks ago I gave B. my essay on Kafka. I'm sure he read it, but he never alluded to it of his own accord, and on two occasions when I steered the conversation round to it he replied evasively. In the end I took the manuscript away again without saying a word. Last night he suddenly began speaking of this essay. The rather abrupt transition took the form of a remark to the effect that I, too, could not be completely acquitted of a diaristic style of writing *à la* Nietzsche. My Kafka essay, for instance. It treated Kafka purely from the phenomenal point of view – the work as something that had grown separately, by itself – the man, too – it detached the work from all connections, even with its author. In the end everything I wrote always came down to the question of *essence*. Now what would be the correct way of tackling the problem of Kafka? The correct way would be to ask: what does he do? how does he behave? And, at the start, to consider the general rather than the particular. It would then transpire that Kafka lived in Prague, in an unhealthy milieu of journalists, of self-important litterati; in that world, literature was the principal reality if not the only one. Kafka's strengths and weaknesses were bound up with this way of seeing the world – his artistic value, but also his feebleness in many respects. He was a Jew-boy – one could just as well coin the term 'Aryan boy' – a sorry, dismal creature, a mere bubble on the glittering quagmire of Prague cultural life, nothing more. Yet there were also some very interesting aspects of him. One could bring these out. One might imagine a conversation between Lao Tzu and the disciple Kafka. Lao Tzu says: 'And so, Disciple Kafka, you have conceived a horror of the organizations, property relations and economic forms within which you live?' – 'Yes.' – 'You can't find your way about them any more?' – 'No.' – 'A share certificate fills you with dread?' – 'Yes.' – 'And so now you're looking for a leader you can hold on to, Disciple Kafka.' 'Of course such an attitude won't do,' says Brecht. 'I don't accept Kafka, you know.' And he goes on to speak about a Chinese philosopher's parable of 'the tribulations of usefulness'. In a wood there are many different kinds of tree-trunk. From the thickest they make ship's timbers; from those which are less thick but still quite sturdy, they make boxes and coffin-lids; the thinnest of all are made into whipping-rods; but of the stunted ones they make nothing at all: these escape the tribulations of usefulness. 'You've got to look around in Kafka's writings as you might in such a wood. Then you'll find a whole lot of very useful things. The images are good, of course. But the rest is pure mystification. It's nonsense. You have to ignore it. Depth doesn't get you anywhere at all. Depth is a separate dimension, it's just depth – and there's nothing whatsoever to be seen in it.' To conclude the discussion I tell B. that penetrating into depth is my way of travelling to the antipodes. In my essay on Kraus I actually got there. I know that the one on Kafka doesn't come off to the same degree: I can't dismiss the charge that it has landed me in a diaristic style of notation. It is true that the study of the frontier area defined by Kraus and, in another way, by Kafka preoccupies me a great deal. In Kafka's case I haven't yet, I said, completed my exploration of this area. I am aware that it contains a lot of rubbish and waste, a lot of pure mystification. But I can't help thinking that the important thing about Kafka is something else, and some of this I touched upon in my essay. B.'s approach should, I said, be checked against interpretations of specific works. I suggested *The Next Village*, and was immediately able to observe the conflict in which this suggestion plunged B. He resolutely rejected Eisler's view that this very short story is 'worthless', but neither could he get anywhere nearer to defining its value. 'One ought to study it more closely,' he said. Then the conversation broke off, as it was ten o'clock and time to listen to the news from Vienna.

31 August. The night before last a long and heated debate about my Kafka. Its foundation: the charge that it promotes Jewish fascism. It increases and spreads the darkness surrounding Kafka instead of dispersing it. Yet it is necessary to clarify Kafka, that is to say to formulate the practicable suggestions which can be extracted from his stories. It is to be supposed that such suggestions *can* be extracted from them, if only because of their tone of superior calm. But these suggestions should be sought in the direction of the great general evils which assail humanity today. Brecht looks for the reflexion of these evils in Kafka's work. He confines himself, in the main, to *The Trial.* What it conveys above all else, he thinks, is a dread of the unending and irresistible growth of the great cities. He claims to know the nightmare of this idea from his own intimate experience. Such cities are an expression of the boundless maze of indirect relationships, complex mutual dependencies and compartmentations into which human beings are forced by modern forms of living. And these in turn find expression in the longing for a 'leader'. The petty bourgeois sees the leader as the only man whom, in a world where everyone can pass the buck to someone else, he can make responsible for all his ills. Brecht calls *The Trial* a prophetic book. 'By looking at the Gestapo you can see what may become of the Cheka.' Kafka's outlook is that of a man caught under the wheels. Odradek is characteristic of this outlook: Brecht interprets the house-porter as personifying the worries of a father of a family. The petty bourgeois is bound to get it in the neck. His situation is Kafka's own. But whereas the type of petty bourgeois current today – that is, the fascist – has decided to set his indomitable iron will against this situation, Kafka hardly opposes it; he is wise. Where the fascist brings heroism into play, Kafka responds with questions. He asks for safeguards for his situation. But the nature of his situation is such that the safeguards he demands must be unreasonable. It is a Kafkaesque irony that the man who appears to be convinced of nothing so much as of the frailty of all safeguards should have been an insurance agent. Incidentally, his unlimited pessimism is free from any tragic sense of destiny. For not only is his expectation of misfortune founded on nothing but empiricism (although it must be said that this foundation is unshakable), but also, with incorrigible naïvety, he seeks the criterion of final success in the most insignificant and trivial undertakings – a visit from a travelling salesman, an inquiry at a government office. For parts of the time the conversation centred on the story *The Next Village.* Brecht says it is a counterpart to the story of Achilles and the tortoise. One never gets to the next village if one breaks the journey down into its smallest parts, not counting the incidental occurrences. Then a whole life is too short for the journey. But the fallacy lies in the word 'one'. For if the journey is broken down into its parts, then the traveller is too. And if the unity of life is destroyed, then so is its shortness. Let life be as short as it may. That does not matter, for the one who arrives in the next village is not the one who set out on the journey, but another. – I for my part offer the following interpretation: the true measure of life is memory. Looking back, it traverses the whole of life like lightning. As fast as one can turn back a few pages, it has travelled from the next village to the place where the traveller took the decision to set out. Those for whom life has become transformed into writing – like the grandfather in the story – can only read the writing backwards. That is the only way in which they encounter themselves, and only thus – by fleeing from the present – can they understand life.

27 September. Dragør. In a conversation a few evenings ago Brecht spoke of the curious indecision which at the moment prevents him from making any definite plans. As he is the first to point out, the main reason for this indecision is that his situation is so much more privileged than that of most other refugees. Therefore, since in general he scarcely admits that emigration can be a proper basis for plans and projects, he refuses all the more radically to admit it as such in his own particular case. His plans reach out to the period beyond emigration. There, he is faced with two alternatives. On the one hand there are some prose projects waiting to be done: the shorter one of the *Ui* – a satire on Hitler in the style of the Renaissance biographers – and the long one of the *Tui* novel. This is to be an encyclopedic survey of the follies of the Tellectual-Ins (intellectuals); it seems that it will be set, in part at least, in China. A small model for this work is already completed. But besides these prose projects he is also preoccupied by others, dating back to very old studies and ideas. Whereas he was able, at a pinch, to set down in his notes and introductions to the *Versuche* the thoughts which occurred to him within the scope of epic theatre, other thoughts, although originating in the same interests, have become combined with his study of Leninism and also of the scientific tendencies of the empiricists, and have therefore outgrown that rather limited framework. For several years past they have been subsumed, now under one key concept, now under another, so that non-Aristotelian logic, behaviourist theory, the new encyclopedia and the critique of ideas have, in turn, stood at the centre of his preoccupations. At present these various pursuits are converging upon the idea of a philosophical didactic poem. But he has doubts about the matter. He wonders, in the first instance, whether, in view of his output to date and especially of its satirical elements, particularly the *Three-penny Novel,* the public would accept such a work. This doubt is made up of two distinct strands of thought. Whilst becoming more closely concerned with the problems and methods of the proletarian class struggle, he has increasingly doubted the satirical and especially the ironic attitude as such. But to confuse these doubts, which are mostly of a practical nature, with other, more profound ones would be to misunderstand them. The doubts at a deeper level concern the artistic and playful element in art, and above all those elements which, partially and occasionally, make art refractory to reason. Brecht's heroic efforts to legitimize art *vis-à-vis* reason have again and again referred him to the parable in which artistic mastery is proved by the fact that, in the end, all the artistic elements of a work cancel each other out. And it is precisely these efforts, connected with this parable, which are at present coming out in a more radical form in the idea of the didactic poem. In the course of the conversation I tried to explain to Brecht that such a poem would not have to seek approval from a bourgeois public but from a proletarian one, which, presumably, would find its criteria less in Brecht's earlier, partly bourgeois-oriented work than in the dogmatic and theoretical content of the didactic poem itself. 'If this didactic poem succeeds in enlisting the authority of Marxism on its behalf,' I told him, 'then your earlier work is not likely to weaken that authority.'

4 October. Yesterday Brecht left for London. Whether it is that my presence offers peculiar temptations in this respect, or whether Brecht is now generally more this way inclined than before, at all events his aggressiveness (which he himself calls 'baiting') is now much more pronounced in conversation than it used to be. Indeed,

I am struck by a special vocabulary engendered by this aggressiveness. In particular, he is fond of using the term *Würstchen* (little sausage). In Dragør I was reading Dostoyevsky's *Crime and Punishment*. To start with he blamed this choice of reading for my being unwell. As confirmation he told how, in his youth, a prolonged illness (which had doubtless been latent for a long time) had begun when a schoolfellow had played Chopin to him on the piano and he had not had the strength to protest. Brecht thinks that Chopin and Dostoyevsky have a particularly adverse effect on people's health. In other ways, too, he missed no opportunity of needling me about my reading matter, and as he himself was reading *Schweyk* at the time he insisted on making comparative value judgements of the two authors. It became evident that Dostoyevsky simply could not measure up to Hašek, and Brecht included him without further ado among the *Würstchen*; only a little more and he would have extended to Dostoyevsky the description he keeps ready, these days, for any work which lacks an enlightening character, or is denied such character by him: he calls such a work a *Klump* (lump, or clot).

1938

28 June. I was in a labyrinth of stairs. This labyrinth was not entirely roofed over. I climbed; other stairways led downwards. On a landing I realized that I had arrived at a summit. A wide view of many lands opened up before me. I saw other men standing on other peaks. One of these men was suddenly seized by dizziness and fell. The dizziness spread; others were now falling from other peaks into the depths below. When I too became dizzy I woke up.

On 22 June I arrived at Brecht's.

Brecht speaks of the elegance and nonchalance of Virgil's and Dante's basic attitude, which, he says, forms the backdrop to Virgil's majestic *gestus*. He calls both Virgil and Dante '*promeneurs*'. Emphasizing the classic rank of the *Inferno*, he says: 'You can read it out of doors.'

He speaks of his deep-rooted hatred of priests, a hatred he inherited from his grandmother. He hints that those who have appropriated the theoretical doctrines of Marx and taken over their management will always form a clerical camarilla. Marxism lends itself all too easily to 'interpretation'. Today it is a hundred years old and what do we find? (At this point the conversation was interrupted.) '"The State must wither away." Who says that? The State.' (Here he can only mean the Soviet Union.) He assumes a cunning, furtive expression, puts himself in front of the chair in which I am sitting – he is impersonating 'the State' –and says, with a sly, sidelong glance at an imaginary interlocutor: 'I know I *ought* to wither away.'

A conversation about new Soviet novels. We no longer read them. The talk then turns to poetry and to the translations of poems from various languages in the USSR with which *Das Wort* is flooded. He says the poets over there are having a hard time. 'If Stalin's name doesn't crop up in a poem, that's interpreted as a sign of ill intent.'

29 June. Brecht talks about epic theatre, and mentions plays acted by children in which faults of performance, operating as alienation effects, impart epic characteristics to the production. Something similar may occur in third-rate provincial theatre. I mention the Geneva production of *Le Cid* where the sight of the king's crown worn crookedly on his head gave me the first inkling of the ideas I eventually developed in the *Trauerspiel* book nine years later. Brecht in turn quoted the moment at which the idea of epic theatre first came into his head. It happened at a rehearsal for the Munich production of *Edward II*. The battle in the play is supposed to occupy the stage for three-quarters of an hour. Brecht couldn't stage-manage the soldiers, and neither could Asya [Lacis], his production assistant. Finally he turned in despair to Karl Valentin, at that time one of his closest friends, who was attending the rehearsal, and asked him: 'Well, what is it? What's the truth about these soldiers? What *about* them?' Valentin: 'They're pale, they're scared, that's what!' The remark settled the issue, Brecht adding: 'They're tired.' Whereupon the soldiers' faces were thickly made up with chalk, and that was the day the production's style was determined.

Later the old subject of 'logical positivism' came up. I adopted a somewhat intransigent attitude and the conversation threatened to take a disagreeable turn. This was avoided by Brecht admitting for the first time that his arguments were superficial. This he did with the delightful formula: 'A deep need makes for a superficial grasp.' Later, when we were walking to his house (the conversation had taken place in my room): 'It's a good thing when someone who has taken up an extreme position then goes into a period of reaction. That way he arrives at a half-way house.' That, he explained, was what had happened to him: he had become mellow.

In the evening: I should like to get somebody to take a small present – a pair of gloves – for Asya. Brecht thinks this might be tricky. It could happen that someone thought the gloves were Jahnn's* way of repaying Asya for her espionage services. 'The worst is always that whole sets of directives† are withdrawn en bloc, but the instructions they contain presumably remain in force.'

1 July. Whenever I refer to conditions in Russia, Brecht's comments are highly sceptical. When I inquired the other day whether Ottwald was still in gaol (in colloquial German: whether he was 'still sitting'), the answer was: 'If he can still sit, he's sitting.' Yesterday Gretl Steffin expressed the opinion that Tretyakov was no longer alive.

4 July. Brecht in the course of a conversation on Baudelaire last night: 'I'm not against the asocial, you know; I'm against the non-social.'

21 July. The publications of Lukács, Kurella *et al* are giving Brecht a good deal of trouble. He thinks, however, that one ought not to oppose them at the theoretical level. I then put the question on the political level. Here he does not hold his punches. 'Socialist economy doesn't need war, and that is why it is opposed to war. The "peace-

---

* The name, presumably that of the proposed intermediary, cannot be deciphered with absolute certainty; perhaps Hans Henny Jahn?
† Uncertain reading of the manuscript.

loving nature of the Russian people" is an expression of this and nothing else. There can't be a socialist economy in one country. Rearmament has inevitably set the Russian proletariat a long way back in history, back to stages of historical development which have long since been overtaken – among others, the monarchic stage. Russia is now under personal rule. Only blockheads can deny this, of course.' This was a short conversation which was soon interrupted. – I should add that in this context Brecht emphasized that as a result of the dissolution of the First International, Marx and Engels lost active contact with the working-class movement and thereafter gave only advice – of a private nature, not intended for publication – to individual leaders. Nor was it an accident – although regrettable – that Engels at the end of his life turned to the natural sciences.

Béla Kun, he said, was his greatest admirer in Russia. Brecht and Heine were the only German poets Kun studied [*sic*]. (Occasionally Brecht hints at the existence of a certain person on the Central Committee who supports him.)

25 July. Yesterday morning Brecht came over to my place to read me his Stalin poem, which is entitled 'The Peasant to his Ox'. At first I did not get its meaning completely, and when a moment later the thought of Stalin passed through my head, I did not dare entertain it. This was more or less the effect Brecht intended, and he explained what he meant in the conversation which followed. In this conversation he emphasized, among other things, the positive aspects of the poem. It was in fact a poem in honour of Stalin, who in his opinion has immense merit. But Stalin is not yet dead. Besides, a different, more enthusiastic manner of honouring Stalin is not incumbent upon Brecht, who is sitting in exile and waiting for the Red Army to march in. He is following the developments in Russia and also the writings of Trotsky. These prove that there exists a suspicion – a justifiable one – demanding a sceptical appraisal of Russian affairs. Such scepticism is in the spirit of the Marxist classics. Should the suspicion prove correct one day, then it will become necessary to fight the regime, and *publicly*. But, 'unfortunately or God be praised, whichever you prefer', the suspicion is at present not yet a certainty. There is no justification for constructing upon it a policy such as Trotsky's. 'And then there's no doubt that certain criminal cliques really are at work in Russia itself. One can see it, from time to time, by the harm they do.' Finally Brecht pointed out that we Germans have been especially affected by the setbacks we have suffered in our own country. 'We have had to pay for the stand we took, we're covered with scars. It's only natural that we should be especially sensitive.'

Towards evening Brecht found me in the garden reading *Capital*. Brecht: 'I think it's very good that you're studying Marx just now, at a time when one comes across him less and less, especially among our people.' I replied that I prefer studying the most talked-about authors when they are out of fashion. We went on to discuss Russian literary policy. I said, referring to Lukács, Gábor and Kurella: 'These people just aren't anything to write home about' [literally: with these people you can't make state]. Brecht: 'Or rather, a State is all you *can* make with them, but not a community. They are, to put it bluntly, enemies of production. Production makes them uncomfortable. You never know where you are with production; production is the unforseeable. You never know what's going to come out. And they themselves don't want to produce. They want to play the *apparatchik* and exercise control over other people. Every one of their criticisms contains a threat.' We then got on to Goethe's novels, I don't remember how; Brecht knows only the *Elective Affinities*. He said that what he admired about it was the author's youthful elegance. When I told him Goethe wrote this novel at the age of sixty, he was very much surprised. The book, he said, had nothing philistine about it. That was a tremendous achievement. He knew a thing or two about philistinism; all German drama, including the most significant works, was stamped with it. I remarked that *Elective Affinities* had been very badly received when it came out. Brecht: 'I'm pleased to hear it. – The Germans are a lousy nation [*ein Scheissvolk*]. It isn't true that one must not draw conclusions from Hitler about Germans in general. In me, too, everything that is German is bad. The intolerable thing about us Germans is our narrow-minded independence. Nowhere was there such a thing as the free cities of the German Reich, like that lousy Augsburg. Lyons was never a free city; the independent cities of the Renaissance were city states. – Lukács is a German by choice. He's got no stuffing left in him, none whatsoever.'

Speaking of *The Most Beautiful Legends of Woynok the Brigand* by Anna Seghers, Brecht praised the book because it shows that Seghers is no longer writing to order. 'Seghers can't produce to order, just as, without an order, I wouldn't even know how to start writing.' He also praised the stories for having a rebellious, solitary figure as their central character.

26 July. Brecht, last night: 'There can't be any doubt about it any longer: the struggle against ideology has become a new ideology.'

29 July. Brecht read to me some polemical texts he has written as part of his controversy with Lukács, studies for an essay which is to be published in *Das Wort*. He asked my advice whether to publish them. As, at the same time, he told me that Lukács's position 'over there' is at the moment very strong, I told him I could offer no advice. 'There are questions of power involved. You ought to get the opinion of somebody from over there. You've got friends there, haven't you?' – Brecht: 'Actually, no, I haven't. Neither have the Muscovites themselves – like the dead.'

3 August. On 29 July in the evening, while we were in the garden, the conversation came round to the question whether a part of the *Children's Songs* cycle should be included in the new volume of poems. I was not in favour because I thought that the contrast between the political and the private poems made the experience of exile particularly explicit, and this contrast would be diminished by the inclusion of a disparate sequence. In saying this I probably implied that the suggestion once again reflected the destructive aspect of Brecht's character, which puts everything in danger almost before it has been achieved. Brecht: 'I know; they'll say of me that I was manic. If the history of our time is handed down to the future, the capacity to understand my mania will be handed down with it. The times we live in will make a backdrop to my mania. But what I should really like would be for people to say about me: he was a *moderate* manic.' – His discovery of moderation, Brecht said, should find expression in the poetry volume: the recognition that life goes on despite Hitler, that there will always be children. He was thinking of the 'epoch without history' of which he speaks in his poem addressed to artists. A few days later he told me he thought the coming of such an epoch more likely than victory over fascism. But then he added, with a vehemence he rarely shows, yet another argument in favour of including the *Children's Songs* in the *Poems from Exile*: 'We must neglect nothing in our struggle against that lot. What they're planning is nothing small, make no mistake about it. They're planning for thirty thousand years ahead. Colossal things. Colossal crimes. They stop at nothing. They're out to destroy everything. Every living cell contracts under their blows. That is why we too must think of everything. They cripple the baby in the mother's womb. We must on no account leave out the children.' While he was speaking like this I felt a power being exercised over me which was equal in strength to the power of fascism – I mean a power that sprang from the depths of history no less deep than the power of the fascists. It was a very curious feeling, and new to me. Then Brecht's thoughts took another turn, which further intensified this feeling I had. 'They're planning devastations on an icy scale. That's why they can't reach agreement with the Church, which is also geared to thousands of years. And they've proletarianized me too. It isn't just that they've taken my house, my fish-pond and my car from me; they've also robbed me of my stage and my audience. From where I stand today I can't, as a matter of principle, admit that Shakespeare's talent was greater than mine. But Shakespeare couldn't have written just for his desk drawer, any more than I can. Besides, he had his characters in front of him. The people he depicted were running around in the streets. He just observed their behaviour and picked out a few traits; there were many others, just as important, that he left out.'

Early August. 'In Russia there is dictatorship *over* the proletariat. We should avoid dissociating ourselves from this dictatorship for as long as it still does useful work for the proletariat – i.e. so long as it contributes towards an agreement between the proletariat and the peasantry, with predominant recognition of proletarian interests.' A few days later Brecht spoke of a 'workers' monarchy', and I compared this organism with certain grotesque sports of nature dredged up from the depths of the sea in the form of horned fish or other monsters.

25 August. A Brechtian maxim: 'Don't start from the good old things but the bad new ones.'

BIBLIOGRAPHICAL NOTES

'What is Epic Theatre?' [First version], first published in *Versuche über Brecht*, 1966, from an unpublished manuscript.

'What is Epic Theatre?' [Second version], first published in *Maß und Wert*, 2, 1939.

'Studies for a Theory of Epic Theatre', first published in *Versuche über Brecht*, 1966, from an unpublished manuscript.

'From the Brecht Commentary', first published in the literary supplement of the *Frankfurter Zeitung*, 6 July 1930.

'A Family Drama in the Epic Theatre', first published in *Die literarische Welt*, 5 February 1932.

'The Country where it is Forbidden to Mention the Proletariat', first published in *Die neue Weltbühne*, 30 June 1938.

'Commentaries on Poems by Brecht': 'On the *Studies*' and 'On the *Handbook for City-dwellers*', first published in *Versuche über Brecht*, 1966, from unpublished manuscripts; 'On the "Legend of the Origin of the . . . Tao Te Ching"', first published in the *Schweizer Zeitung am Sonntag*, 23 April 1939; all other commentaries, first published in Walter Benjamin, *Schriften*, vol. 2, Frankfurt, 1955.

'Brecht's *Threepenny Novel*', first published in *Bertolt Brechts Dreigroschenbuch*, Frankfurt, 1960.

'The Author as Producer', first published in *Versuche über Brecht*, 1966, from an unpublished manuscript.

'Conversations with Brecht', first published in *Versuche über Brecht*, 1966, from an unpublished manuscript.

INDEX